# BLACK CHINOOK

## An Army Ranger's Story

ISBN-10  1-60145-011-7
ISBN-13  978-1-60145-011-1

Library of Congress Control Number:  2006907226

References to classified military capabilities and relationships have been removed from *Black Chinook* to protect U.S. Army Rangers on current and future battlefields.

Cover photograph courtesy of 1SG David G. Fraembs.

Printed in the United States of America.

Bouna Books, LLC.
2006

David A. Combs
www.RangerCombs.com

# Black Chinook

An Army Ranger's Story

**DAVID A. COMBS**

# Dedication

To my wife Nyra, my sweetheart and the love of my life, for her

unwavering support of my career as an Army Ranger.

To my parents, Florian and Theresa Combs,

for their inspiration, encouragement, and support.

To my daughter Leilani who grew up without me because

I was almost never home.  My duties kept me on the move.

HALO, my bullmastiff; my second born.

# Acknowledgements

There are many people who had an enduring effect on shaping my life and providing me invaluable skills that helped me to complete my career as a U.S. Army Ranger.

My parents, Florian (Bud) and Theresa (Sidla) Combs. They were the absolute model of dedicated parents and set an example for discipline and moral ethics that were of the highest standard. If I could be half the man my father was, I would be more than prepared to make a very positive and lasting impact on the world. I owe everything to them.

My brothers and sisters: Colleen, Sharon, Jeff, Tom, and Michelle. They were each a very special part of the developmental years of my life. They may have tried to "get me" before I got old enough to talk but the survival instinct they instilled in me served me well.

My lifelong friend Douglas Fenske - we grew up and joined the Army together. We would stay together in the Rangers for six years until our careers took different paths. We would run into each other from Haiti to Afghanistan. No matter where we were - Doug was always my Ranger Buddy.

# Memorial To My Father

Florian Vance Combs
Serial Number: 730-62-28
D.O.W. – Duration of the War
United States Navy
March 19, 1945

*LCS 113 in Saipan, 1945.*

I was a senior in high school and subject to draft upon graduation. I always wanted to join the Navy and joined in March of my senior year. The folks were pretty upset, being an only child, but they were pretty proud and attended the graduation ceremony to receive my diploma … the teachers accelerated all my classes so my grades were earned before I left.

I attended boot camp at Camp Hall, Great Lakes, Illinois and was assigned to LCS113. I was on ship APA38 from San Diego to Samar, Philippines where we were put ashore. Seven of us were flown to Fleet Headquarters on Guam and then via destroyer to Okinawa. It was during this trip that we were in the typhoon that the book "Caine Mutiny" was written about.

The atom bomb was dropped while we were at sea. We were flown to Saipan and the Tinian Islands where we caught a plane flying to Yokahoma in time for the surrender ceremony where the Japanese surrendered to MacArthur on the battleship Missouri (General Douglas MacArthur).

We spent months sweeping and destroying mines in the Korean Straits operating out of Sasebo, Japan. We brought the LCS (Landing Craft Support ship) to Pearl Harbor into dry dock and then on to Astoria, Oregon where it was decommissioned.

On Samar, Saipan and Okinawa we ran into Japanese soldiers who didn't know the war was over and were still resisting. On Samar they wounded one of our guys and on Saipan and Okinawa they were subdued before any damage was done.

It was six months from the time I shipped out from San Diego to the time I got my first mail. All the packages that had been sent were either lost or stolen. I can remember arranging the mail chronologically before I opened it.

I was discharged at the U.S. Navy Station in Minneapolis, Minnesota.

# Table of Contents

# Foreward

I wrote this book at the request of my mother. She had read my letters from around the world for many years but did not fully understand my duties and responsibilities. *Black Chinook* took ten years to write and is a compilation of the events and experiences that have shaped my career as a U.S. Army Officer. I have portrayed these events as accurately as possible from memory, pictures, letters, emails, and old notes. Throughout, I have tried to maintain the integrity of different sections written at different stages of my career.

My Army career was unique in many ways. Over a twenty year period I had the opportunity to see world events unfold from a unique perspective. I was a member of the inner circle of Joint Service planning cells where missions in the interest of the United States of America were conceived, coordinated, and executed. I served in the Special Operations community for seven years and as a POW/MIA Team Leader in Southeast Asia. This provided me insight and an opportunity to impact one of the most politically charged issues affecting the American public since the Vietnam War.

My experiences in this book provide views from the enlisted soldier, Non-Commissioned Officer and Commissioned Officer sides of service. This includes experience based on more advanced schooling and training than most soldiers could hope for in a career. It is my intent to bring a public awareness to a variety of behind the scenes operations, both operational and political.

There is an underlying theme that any reader of this book should take away. On any given day and night of your life, thousands of America's sons and daughters are sacrificing personal safety, aspirations, family, and sometimes their lives, to ensure the security of the United States of America and our way of life. These soldiers are a minority of Americans who have taken the step to make a difference for their generation. The country should be thankful for their service.

\*     \*     \*

During my service in the 75$^{th}$ Ranger Regiment many comrades fell in training and in combat. The *Black Chinook* is an old Ranger based metaphor representing the image of the black Specter of Death coming to remove a fallen Ranger from the battlefield. The courage to serve in the special operations community comes at great personal risk. This telling celebrates the sacrifice of the fallen before they were taken by the *Black Chinook*.

\*     \*     \*

**References to classified military capabilities and relationships have been removed from *Black Chinook* to protect U.S. Army Rangers on current and future battlefields.**

# Dark Operations

The aircraft shuddered as it banked violently to the left. Inside twenty-eight Army Rangers grabbed for any handhold to steady themselves as they waited on one knee for the aircraft to reach its target. Since we had gone "feet dry" off the ocean the lights had been blackened to eliminate any possibility of the enemy targeting the helicopters. As we skimmed the treetops at 100 knots, the only light inside the aircraft came from the dull green glow of the pilot's control panel. The pilots themselves flew with night vision goggles to see through the darkness.

I heard through my headset, "*Check Point four!*" and the helicopter banked hard to the right. I had the luxury of sitting on a step next to the cabin bulkhead. The lurch of the aircraft caused my left shoulder to bump into the Door Gunner. Instantly, an elbow to the head told me to stay the hell out of the way. The gunner struggled to keep his space behind the 7.62mm coaxial machine gun. I took off the headset and handed it back to the Company Commander sitting to my right. He had just finished putting on his gear and wanted to listen to the pilots jabber on the radio. I quickly returned the handmike of my personal tactical radio to my ear and heard it squawk, "*Raven sees the target at four nautical miles ... pushing ahead to engage.*" The two Special Operations attack helicopters rushed forward past our CH-53 Pavlo helicopters. They would attack the barracks and arms room of the Command Post as planned.

"*Dancer on one!*" That meant the team of AH-6 Little Bird helicopters had also made it to the target. The Little Birds would take out the guard tower and the machine guns in bunkers number three and four. Those machineguns faced the little clearing where these pilots planned to land two very large birds at one time.

Dancer Two roared forward and followed the lead of his wingman, *"Dancer One has ... umber ... squaaawk."* *"Dancer Two has four!"* Dancer One took out bunker four with his 2.75 inch rockets then banked hard to the left to avoid flying directly over a trenchline. Dancer Two fired his 7.62 coaxial machine gun and the hail of bullets rained into the guard tower. With a quick bank to the right he placed his "spot" on the bunker and triggered two more rockets. The distinctive whoosh of the rocket motors engaging, to launch the rockets forward, was followed by loud explosions as they impacted the target. Dancer Two also banked hard to the left to avoid enemy fire.

A half-mile to the north Raven Three One and Three Two were on their second attack of the barracks and arms room. The quick metallic crack of the twin .50 caliber machine guns firing, followed by the whoosh of rockets streaking toward their targets, meant it would be a "Hot" objective.

The Load Master screamed, "ONE MINUTE!" This announcement meant we were to prepare to get off his aircraft. The mass of bodies thrown off-balance inside the Pavlo echoed his command. The nose of the aircraft rose as the pilot quickly reduced speed. With intense concentration he attempted to clear the trees on both sides of the aircraft. The distinctive metallic roar of a door gun meant the right Door Gunner had found a target as the aircraft made final adjustments above the trees. The chopper could not land, so it flattened out, and came to a hover.

Over the roar of the door guns engaging targets, the Load Master now screamed, "FAST ROPE, FAST ROPE, FAST ROPE!" The Rangers quickly slung their weapons over their backs, donned their leather gloves, stood, and moved toward the open ramp. The Load Master had just finished kicking out the two large wool ropes that now dangled the fifty feet to the ground. A chemical light was attached to the end of the rope and he peered over the edge of the ramp to ensure the light was on the ground. Once confirmed he commanded, "GO! GO! GO!" One at a time, the Rangers grasped the top of the rope firmly, and stepped off the ramp into the black of night.

One after the other the men slid toward the ground. The friction burned into their leather gloves as speed increased under the weight of individual equipment. Each Ranger's spiral to the ground ended in a bone-jarring grunt. It was imperative you hit the ground and rolled out of the way. Otherwise, the next man off the rope threatened to land on your head.

Once on the ground, the Rangers quickly moved to the west end of the clearing. They waited until the first fire team was assembled and then pushed off to the south of the target. The roar of the two Pavlos, departing over our heads, drowned out all but bursts from the Door Gunner. There were no tracers used as they would reveal the location of the aircraft in the sky. This could easily invite more than its share of enemy fire. It was no coincidence that the night was so dark. It was a new moon and the suspected illumination was 3% - no illumination made it difficult for the enemy to see.

I whispered into my handmike, "*Dancer ... this is Charlie Zero ... SITREP*" as I tripped on some barbed wire and fell on my face. I needed to establish contact with the Dancer aircraft.

The AH-6 Little Birds replied, "*Dancer has bunkers 3 and 4 destroyed, guard tower destroyed, no lights on objective ... holding in Orbit One.*"

Again I whispered into my handmike, "*Charlie Zero ... Good Copy ... Raven Two One, Two Two ... SITREP*"

"*Raven has barracks and arms room destroyed ... two BRDMs burning ... holding Orbit Two.*"

"*Good copy Raven ... Charlie Zero out.*"

A strong hand grabbed the back of my body armor and pulled my face from the dirt. The Company Commander commanded, "Let's go FSO!"

With my head out of the dirt I announced, "Sir, Bunkers 3 and 4 and the guard tower are destroyed. No lights on the objective. The reaction force on Objective Viking destroyed!"

The commander replied, "Good ... Let's move!"

The second lift of Pavlo helicopters now roared to our rear as fifty more Rangers slid to the ground. The first lift had carried the support position and the breach team. The second lift carried the assault teams. A massive roar of automatic and anti-tank weapons fire erupted about a hundred meters to my right. It was the support position opening up with new M240G machine guns, Carl Gustav anti-tank guns and 60 mm mortars.

*"Charlie Zero November in position!"* came from the earpiece of my handmike. My Fire Support Sergeant had reached the support position and had a good view of the target. I huffed a reply into the handmike as I ran, *"Raven in Orbit 2, Dancer in Orbit 1... take control."*

*"Roger out!"* he replied. I could hear Charlie Zero November tell both sets of attack helicopters to reengage their targets.

To the naked eye there was nothing out of the ordinary on our side of the objective. When I looked through my night vision goggles, the objective was crisscrossed with infrared (IR) laser pointers. Platoon and Squad leaders were pointing out targets to the gunners in the false security of the darkness. "Local support, let's go!" an NCO half yelled. Immediately, two M240G and two SAW 5.56mm machine guns opened up from the edge of the tree line. They directed their fire into bunkers on our side of the objective. Green tracers streaked the fifty meters to the enemy bunkers and kicked up dirt and debris as they ate away at the sandbags.

The Platoon Sergeant yelled, "BREACH TEAM, GO!" and two Rangers immediately sprang from the woods. They ran and crawled between a twenty meter steel gauntlet of bullets as the tracers streamed on each side of them. Seconds later they were near the bunkers as one man fired at the trench line and the other rammed a field expedient Bangalore torpedo into the wire. A flash of an orange chemical light meant the fuse had been pulled and the two Rangers scrambled their way back to the tree line.

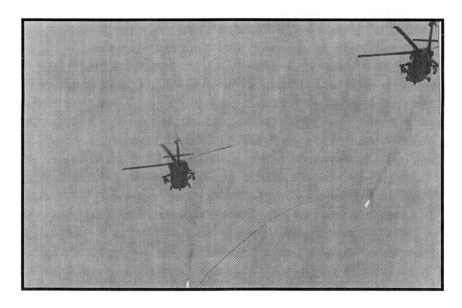

As I needed to be heard above the machine guns, I yelled into the radio, "*Raven and Dancer clear to Orbits One and Two ... Demo Out!*"

"*Raven and Dancer are clearing to orbits.*" the Flight Lead called back.

The guns continued to blaze. The Commander counted down the fuze time, "Eight ... seven ... six ... get your heads down!" A huge explosion erupted from the concertina wire and dust billowed as rocks and gravel rained down around us.

Both teams of attack helicopters announced over the radio net, *"Raven and Dancer inbound."* Moments later the first set of attack helicopters cleared the trees and immediately engaged the bunkers and trench line near the breach. The assault team broke from the tree line and sprinted through the gauntlet. In seconds they had entered the trenches. *"Assault in the wire!"* was the call on all radio nets. The support position and attack helicopters then shifted their fires to the north half of the objective. The assault team would clear the trench line on the south half and work their way to the command center.

The point man in the trench rounded a corner and met the enemy soldier face to face. At point blank range, the point-man loosed a round of double ott buckshot from his 12-gauge sawed-off shotgun. The impact of the pellets left a large hole in the enemy soldier's chest as it drove him backwards to the ground.

Streaking rockets and their resulting explosions echoed from seventy meters north. The attack helicopters were taking direction from the Forward Observers who moved just behind the lead fire teams. The observer controlled the close air support, *"Dancer Two One this is Charlie Five Three. From my position at bunker number three, marked by IR strobe ... direction 350 degrees, 70 meters, enemy infantry."* The Forward Observer then directed an invisible beam of laser light with his IR Laser Pointer directly onto the target as he looked through his night vision goggles.

*"Dancer Two One inbound ... I have your position ... I have your mark."* replied the pilot almost robotically.

*"You are cleared hot!"* yelled the Forward Observer over the roar of the gunfire. A trail of tracers streaked from the outline of the aircraft above us followed by the sound of rockets streaking forward and exploding on the target. The observer

then adjusted the fire by announcing, *"Dancer Two Two ... north fifty!"*

*"Dancer Two Two has your mark."* The now familiar screech of streaking rockets was followed by the deep thumping explosion of the warhead. The echo and vibration of metal impacting metal resounded through the night like a deep bass drum.

A Squad Leader announced, "Clearing team up!" Seconds later a team of four Rangers ran to the side of a building and stacked in a line near the door. Two rooms down the building was the right limit of the machine gun team. The machine gun team was pouring lead into the building to ensure anyone who was still alive would not have a chance to get off a shot at the clearing team. The lead man of the clearing team blew the dead bolt and handles off the door with his shotgun. Then kicked open the door. Three seconds later the whole team had entered the hallway, blown the handle off the first door and entered the first room.

This was a textbook and intense Special Operations mission that never found its way into the newspapers. There were friendly casualties, huge amounts of aircraft, personnel and ammunition expended and no one would ever know it had occurred. Three U.S. Army Rangers were casualties that night. One man was shot through the thigh by a machine gun. The second Ranger took buckshot pellets in the neck, and the third had buckshot embedded in his arm.

These were the casualties of readiness - the acceptable losses to ensure national security. To the Special Operations community the death or injury of a comrade is a common occurrence. Physically debilitating and life altering injuries are extremely common. The rest of the nation had no idea that on a dark night in 1994, a Company of U.S. Army Rangers had raided and destroyed a replica third world Command Post

located in the backwoods of Georgia. The enemy consisted of
target silhouettes ... the Ranger casualties were real.

# Chapter 1
## In The Beginning

W hen I was seven years old, my family moved from Minneapolis to the town of Cresco in Northeast Iowa. I primarily grew up on a farm and over the years spent countless days in the woods by myself tracking deer and imagining life as a mountain man. My only diversion from the farm was school and playing football. From football I learned the value of teamwork and I enjoyed the violent competition. These lessons were utterly invaluable in the preparation for everything to come in my life. I remember my High School football coach, Bill Kosters, saying one day outside of the weight room, "You guy's have got to be tough; it's just like if you have to go to war someday; you have to step up." I did not realize how prophetic those words would be.

After graduating from Northeast Missouri State University in Kirksville, in May of 1985, I skipped the graduation, and headed home to the farm. I had a Bachelor of Science Degree to my credit and was determined to land a job as soon as possible. I sent out twenty resumes and soon had an interview scheduled with a major agricultural firm, Pioneer Seed Corn. I arrived at the interview early, looked good, and felt confident a job would be mine in short fashion. The interviewer began by saying, "I see it took you five years to get your degree and your GPA dropped from 3.45 to 2.66. How do you explain that?" At that point, I knew the interview was not looking good.

During my senior year of college, a series of events occurred which altered my plans for the rest of my life. I had religiously watched the coverage of the Grenada Invasion on the television. I listened intently to the accounts of Army Rangers parachuting onto the island. A television documentary on Ranger training aired that same week and whetted my appetite even more. Later, my dad mentioned one of my uncles had been a Ranger in WWII and had participated in a raid on a prison camp. Then the movie *Red Dawn* found its way into the house and pushed me over the edge. My interest in joining the Army had peaked. The time was right and I just needed to take the step and get on with it.

I walked into the nearest Army Recruiting Office in Decorah, Iowa, and said I wanted to be an Army Ranger. Sergeant First Class Dennis Landis sat behind his desk, raised an eyebrow, and had me fill out a questionnaire. As he picked up the completed questionnaire, his eyebrow raised again. He obviously felt he had hit the jackpot. I was a college graduate, in good shape, who wanted to enlist as soon as possible.

Two days later I was on my way to Fort Des Moines, to an Army Reception Station, to determine my options for a military specialty. I took the Army Skills Vocational Aptitude Battery (ASVAB) which was used to determine your potential to succeed in a variety of army Military Occupational Specialties. I scored 123 out of a possible 130 points and was informed my score was well beyond the 110 points required to qualify for any job in the Army. I then awaited my turn in front of the computer which listed the available Army jobs.

The recruiter said, "Sorry bud, there are no Ranger slots open - how about something else?" I think they saw me as overconfident as I had specifically asked for a Ranger slot and they thought I was full of myself. After all, I was just another guy off the block wanting to join the Army.

I replied, "No deal. It's Ranger or nothing!" I was intent on finding something special or nothing at all. Nothing of interest was offered and I was excused to a waiting room. Thirty minutes later, a tall Non-Commissioned Officer came to the waiting room and said he had something to show me. "How about being a Ranger Fire Support Specialist?" he said.

I asked, "A what?"

He told me to look at a television screen and clicked in a VCR tape. Soon a film started which showed a M577 Command Post armored vehicle running around the countryside and setting up antennas.

"Is that in a Ranger Battalion?" I asked.

He answered, "Yep, you go to Basic Training, Advanced Individual Training, Airborne School, and then straight to the Rangers."

"I'll take it!" I would be required to sign a four year contract as an Unassigned Ranger. I would not know until after six months into the training what my final destination would be. I did know it would be in the 75th Ranger Regiment—that was all I cared about. If I failed at any step of the training process, I would be subject to worldwide reassignment at the needs of the Army.

Looking back, it was apparent the recruiters at the Reception Station had no idea what they were talking about when it came to the Ranger Battalions. By sheer accident I got the job I wanted from watching a bogus tape. Over the years to come, a lack of military and public knowledge of the Ranger Regiment would be reinforced time and again.

My plans upset my parents. Florian (Bud) and Theresa Combs were extremely hardworking mid-western conservative folks who saw politics and world events from a very practical perspective. The military had been a huge part of my family and had captured my imagination during my childhood. My Uncle Jim Kautz was in France in World War I and during one visit to his farm he showed me a picture of himself in the trenches. During WWII my father served proudly in the Navy in the Pacific Theater on LCS 113. My mother had four brothers and a sister in the various services at one time. I still think of my Uncle Stan Sidla who was a Marine in the Pacific and fought a little known battle to hold a hilltop. I heard that story so many times as a child that I could close my eyes and *see* him shooting savagely at waves of attacking Japanese. Later he would crawl down among the bodies to rummage for ammunition and water to last until relief finally came days later. Uncle Stan survived the ordeal and was decorated for the action.

At the back of the family shoe store my dad sat down with me and carefully explained his reservations about my choice to join the Army. As my mother listened from the next room, he sat with a pencil in his right hand and looked me directly in the eye as I sat on a chair to his left. To this day I can remember his words. "David, no father hopes to see his son go off to war or to make a career out of killing people. I felt I went to war so my sons would not have to." He also explained that our family had always served, but the only way he could see it supporting a future for my family was to someday become an officer. I listened intently to what my father said, but I told him my decision had been made—I was joining the Army. From that point on my parents supported me one-hundred percent and consistently wrote me wherever my service took me.

Once my plans were settled I informed my buddy Doug Fenske. Doug had been working at a local trailer factory and decided to enlist also. At the time, the Army offered a buddy program where two friends could join together and stay together through Basic Training and Advanced Individual Training. So that was it and we joined on the buddy system for four years of adventure as Army Rangers.

\*     \*     \*

**A**rmy Green. Doug and I arrived at Fort Sill, Oklahoma, on 24 August 1985. We carried our bags through the stifling heat and moved into the Reception Station with around two-hundred new recruits from across the nation. This diverse group of men would affect my life for the next three months. We would eat, sleep, sweat, and train as a team to become soldiers. At the time, the experience of Basic Training and Advanced Individual Training was an unknown and therefore a big challenge. In retrospect, what had been challenging and stressful only gave us the minimum preparedness for life as a truly professional soldier. For most soldiers it was the most demanding and shocking experience of their lives. For Doug and me it was the first step in a long road of training to reach our final goal of becoming Army Rangers.

As we poured out the doors of the "cattle car," Drill Sergeants with round brimmed hats greeted us with incoherent screams. We were made to do pushups and mountain climbers in the street and on the sidewalk to create confusion. The Drill Sergeants wanted to see how we would react. As others got tired and reached muscle failure, I continued to knock out pushups and do mountain climbers in a big pool of my own sweat. Finally, a Drill Sergeant commanded, "A'ten ... shun!" I popped up and stood still as a rock and stared straight ahead. I had actually practiced this in the mirror at the shoe store. Drill Sergeants were saying intimidating things into my ear but I remained solid. They were also sizing me up. Prior to my arrival at basic training I had been on a beer and pizza diet mixed in with lifting weights. Due to my size and my age I must have made a good impression. I heard a voice say, "Where is he going?"
Another voice answered, "Fourth Platoon."

5

Then Drill Sergeant, Sergeant First Class (SFC) Winisko, appeared in front of me, looked me in the eye, and told me I would be his Platoon Guide. I had no idea what that meant. SFC Winisko explained. I would be in charge of carrying out his guidance and direction to the rest of the platoon of thirty-four soldiers. It was my job to make sure all tasks were accomplished to standard and I would be the focal point for retribution.

It became obvious that recruits were affected differently based on the environment they had come from. Basic Training had the greatest effect upon the young soldier who did not have a respect for authority. That type of individual got "special" attention and had a rough experience. Under constant scrutiny by our Drill Sergeants, the slightest error by anyone within the platoon resulted in group physical suffering. Peer pressure was intense and infighting and bickering common.

Regardless of how much help some soldiers received, they always seemed to be substandard and the entire group paid the price. Many times soldiers asked me if they could do a "blanket party" on an individual. A "blanket party" consisted of a group attacking a soldier when he was asleep, holding him down, and beating the crap out of him with soap inside pillow cases. The "party" sent the message that the platoon was sick and tired of paying the price for his shortcomings. I was the Platoon Guide, older and bigger, and therefore I guess any clearance for that action had to come through me. There were certainly a couple of soldiers that irritated me, but in reality no one had deserved such treatment. In the end, there were no actual blanket parties in my platoon. We did have to physically impress upon two of our soldiers that they couldn't get away with smoking in the latrine or not keeping themselves clean. I never understood how someone could not know their body was nasty to the point they grossed out everyone else. It was made clear to clean yourself or the platoon would ensure you did. That option would not be comfortable.

During our training at Fort Sill, the Drill Sergeants were very professional, and I had the utmost respect for their experience and their dedication to the task of training us. Under their mentorship we worked as a team to become stronger physically, learn our weapons and equipment, and acquire the discipline required of professional soldiers. The group worked well together and some of the weaker soldiers made great strides in improving themselves. Before we knew it, Basic Training was over and we began the Advanced Individual Training (AIT). During this phase we learned twenty-percent of our basic job. We would all be trained as 13F (Thirteen Fox) Forward Observers. We would be responsible for calling and adjusting all forms of fire support: artillery, mortar, naval gunfire, close-air and attack helicopters.

During AIT there was a shift to a more academic environment. We spent long hours in Snow Hall learning how to call for and adjust artillery fire and to operate communications equipment. These skills would be our bread and butter. We also honed basic skills like land navigation and rappelling. AIT was not hard but sometimes I was just too smart (or dumb) for my own good. I asked questions that would make the instructor stop and look at me with a puzzled gaze. I was just trying to figure out *why* we did it that way.

Looking back years later, after training countless Forward Observers myself, I can see their frustration. There are some procedures that are just executed; to explain *why* required an understanding of all phases of artillery. Most Non-Commissioned Officers were experts in one of the three phases of artillery. Usually only Commissioned Officers were trained in all three phases. The course climaxed with a live-fire demonstration and the graded adjustment of live artillery rounds.

Before we knew it, it was time to move on. The members of our platoon were scattered across the Army. Each of us had a different idea of what we expected to accomplish in the military. Many soldiers were in the Army to collect college money, fulfill their Reserve Officers' Training Corps (ROTC) or West Point commitment, or to find occupational security with the least amount of discomfort. There were places within the military to accommodate those soldiers. There were also units where the adventurous could go to test their mettle.

\*      \*      \*

**S**torm Troopers. Doug and I left Fort Sill on a clear and cool day in December 1985. After a flight connection in St. Louis, we arrived in Columbus, Georgia. We gathered our checked baggage, loaded into a taxi, and drove twenty minutes to Fort Benning, the home of the U.S. Army Airborne School. The weather was similar to Oklahoma and the smell of the pine forests was in the air.

On the first day of training we received an orientation brief from the Airborne School Cadre Commander. He addressed the entire class of over three-hundred assembled soldiers: "Airborne candidates! Look at the man to your left ... look at the man to your right. Fifty percent of you will not be here for graduation day. Some of you will get hurt. Some of you will quit. That's just the way it is."

Airborne School is a threshold within the Army which makes every candidate feel like they are a part of something special—a cut above the average "leg" soldier. There is nothing wrong with a soldier who elected to avoid the airborne option. Mechanized infantry and armor units are powerful and proven killing forces with colorful and proud heritages. However, it is the fact that as an individual, you have taken a step to go above and beyond that makes you feel special.

Each Airborne candidate felt a nervous energy because he had challenged himself and taken the risk to fail or succeed. Failure could result in embarrassment as you attempted to explain failure to your family and unit. However, success injected each new paratrooper with confidence and pride. They had earned the right to join the ranks of a proud lineage of paratroopers.

The course was broken into three phases: Ground Week, Tower Week and Jump Week. The phases progressed in difficulty to give a thorough orientation to your equipment, landing techniques, parachute control techniques, actions in the air and in the aircraft, and exiting the aircraft. The focus was on attention to detail and the safe conduct of airborne operations.

I'll never forget my first five parachute jumps at 1,200 feet. The first was from a C-130 Hercules, a four engine propeller airplane, and the remaining four from a C-141 Starlifter, a larger four-engine jet plane. At the time these were the work horses of the Air Force. As I sat in the aircraft and it began its run down the runway, I was filled with nervous anticipation. My stomach let me know that all the trash talk in the world didn't mean a thing now. It was a short and direct flight to Fryar Drop Zone on the Alabama side of Fort Benning. Sooner than expected, the Jumpmaster began his series of jump commands. "Stand Up, Hook Up, Check Equipment and Sound Off for Equipment Check!" These commands got all jumpers on their feet, hooked up and ready to exit the aircraft. "Stand By ... GO!"

Every paratrooper looking out that door at the ground far below felt a slight pause in his feet. Then the mind willed the body to exit that door into nothingness. For four long seconds your body was blasted by wind and floating in weightlessness. Suddenly a sharp tug on the back, followed by a groin-wrenching stop, let you know your parachute canopy had deployed. Now you floated toward a controlled collision with the ground.

The horror stories told about the Airborne School are somewhat overblown, with the exaggeration depending on how much of a challenge it was to the individual. To me it was no more than a structured environment where a minimal amount of Physical Training (PT), combined with many hours of instruction, prepared you for your first jump from a perfectly good airplane. Considerable embellishment surrounded the Gig

Pit in particular. Every student who had a deficiency in performance, conduct, or uniform quality (spit shined boots and pressed uniform) did not meet the standards and was therefore given a gig. That gig was a mandatory free pass to the pit where tough and punishing PT would take place. It was no big deal and most airborne candidates in the pit actually enjoyed the chance to have a change in the PT routine.

The course lasted for three weeks, culminating with your fifth static line parachute jump and the awarding of your Silver Basic Parachutist Wings. The awarding of the wings took place on the drop zone after the final jump and the procedure was very simple. The wings were pounded against your chest to make the pins on the back puncture your skin. This left two perfect holes oozing blood onto your shirt. Hence the affectionate term of blood wings—every paratrooper's proudest moment.

The Company Commander's prediction had held true. Fifty percent of the students were all that remained for graduation. The other fifty percent failed for a variety of reasons: quitting, lack of nerves, injury, safety violations, or not being able to complete the runs to standard.

\*      \*      \*

That afternoon when many soldiers were headed off to other posts around the world, two Ranger Non-Commissioned Officers (NCOs) arrived at the Airborne School. They were to escort 124 of us to the Ranger Indoctrination Program (RIP) barracks. It was immediately apparent that the Ranger Battalion was a special place. These two NCOs looked sharp and imposing as they stood with their starched jungle fatigues, highly polished jungle boots, shaved heads and coveted black berets—impeccable—professional.

We ran the half-mile to the RIP compound, and for the next three weeks had to prove our worth to the Ranger Regiment. It was made crystal clear the Regiment did not want anything but the best soldiers. It was perfectly acceptable for each and every candidate in the class to fail.

For the next three weeks we endured long hours of Physical Training, hand-to-hand combat, swim tests, road marches, land navigation, parachute jumps, and patrolling through the back woods of Fort Benning. We listened to many accounts of Ranger heroism and sacrifice from past deeds and it set the tone for what we could expect when we arrived at a Ranger Battalion.

The Ranger lineage is steeped in a colorful history and has set the standard for the Rangers of today. Major Robert Rogers Standing Orders from the French and Indian Wars are a cornerstone of every Ranger Handbook and still fundamentally applicable.

## <u>Rogers' Rangers Standing Orders</u>

*1. Don't forget nothing.*
*2. Have your musket clean as a whistle, hatchet scoured, sixty rounds powder and ball, and be ready to march at a minutes warning.*
*3. When you're on the march, act the way you would if you was sneaking up on a deer. See the enemy first.*
*4. Tell the truth about what you see and what you do. There is an army depending on us for correct information. You can lie all you please when you tell other folks about the Rangers, but don't ever lie to a Ranger or an officer.*
*5. Don't ever take a chance you don't have to.*
*6. When you're on the march we march as a single file, far enough apart so one shot can't go thru two men.*
*7. If we strike swamps, or soft ground, we spread out abreast, so it's hard to track us.*
*8. When we march, we keep moving 'til dark, so as to give the enemy the least chance at us.*
*9. When we camp, half the party stays awake while the other half sleeps.*
*10. If we take prisoners, we keep 'em separate 'til we have had time to examine them, they can cook up a story between 'em.*
*11. Don't ever march the same way. Take a different route so you won't be ambushed.*
*12. No matter whether we travel in big parties or little ones, each party has to keep a scout 20 yards ahead, 20 yards on each flank and 20 yards in the rear, so the main body can't be surprised and wiped out.*
*13. Every night you'll be told where to meet if surrounded by a superior force.*
*14. Don't sit down to eat without posting sentries.*

*15. Don't sleep beyond dawn. Dawn's when the French and Indians attack.*
*16. Don't cross a river by a regular ford.*
*17. If somebody's trailing you, make a circle, come back onto your own tracks, and ambush the folks that aim to ambush you.*
*18. Don't stand up when the enemy's coming against you. Kneel down, lie down, or hide behind a tree.*
*19. Let the enemy come 'til he's almost close enough to touch. Then let him have it and jump out and finish him with your hatchet.*

*Major Robert Rogers,*
*1759*

The training was intense and kept the pressure on all Ranger candidates to rise to the occasion or terminate themselves. Each task was new and increased the level of pain based tolerance each candidate could endure of overcome. I'll never forget doing the water confidence course at Victory pond in February. There was ice around the edges of the pond and freezing temperatures in general. The confidence course consisted of the 15-meter swim, log walk, rope drop and slide for life, in that order.

When it was my turn, I jumped backwards off the bank into the water and momentarily went completely under the surface. When I bobbed to the top, I'm sure my lips were already blue— it was freezing! As I struggled to catch my breath, I swam hard with my weapon, LBE (equipment belt of ammo pouches, full canteens and compass), uniform and boots. Before I could get to the end, my legs became so cold that I started to cramp up. I made a few last hard pulls with my arms and reached the ladder.

I handed up the equipment and was pulled from the water by two other Ranger candidates.

I heard someone yell, "Keep Moving Ranger!" and I headed off to the log walk, rope drop and slide for life. I ran to the log walk, climbed the ladder and walked across the thirty foot beam suspended twenty feet above the water. At the end of the beam, I grabbed a taut horizontal rope, climbed twenty feet out onto it, and slapped a RANGER sign. After slapping the sign, I let myself hang and then fall the twenty foot distance into the water. I quickly swam to the shore, and then ran to the slide for life.

The "slide for life" consisted of climbing forty feet up a ladder into a tower, grabbing a set of handles attached to a pulley, and then riding the pulley down a diagonal cable to the water below. Before you got to the end you had to let go of the handles and crash into the water. As I grabbed the handles with my wet and sandy hands, I remember thinking that it would suck to fall off.

As the weeks went by in RIP the pressure increased. Ranger Candidates voluntarily terminated in small groups as they lost their nerve or were injured in training. That was a lesson to be learned—no quitter wanted to "go" alone. They always wanted to take someone else with them. The fear of not completing the course was real for everyone who coveted their black beret. No one wanted to fail and have to explain to their friends and family why they couldn't make the grade.

Two NCOs were extremely memorable. Staff Sergeant (SSG) Lowe was a guy continually sneaking up on candidates and jumping them when their guard was down. I was on barracks guard late one night and stopped in the latrine to relieve myself. I thought I heard something but dismissed it because it was so faint. As I walked out of the latrine, something made me throw my hand up and I caught SSG

Lowe's hand an inch from my face. He let me know I had failed my mission and that the lives of everyone sleeping in the barracks had been compromised because of my error. That lesson has stuck with me to this day. Execute every mission, no matter how menial it seems to you, to the best of your ability.

SSG Scircca was an Arian-looking dude with a bad attitude who had won the Best Ranger Competition the year before. He was extremely physical and enjoyed coming into the compound at odd hours to inflict as much pain on the candidates as he could through exercise. He claimed to be a Druid and Satan worshipper. I heard him ask a student one day, "What do you get from God that I don't get from Satan?"

SSG Scircca was also in charge of the "Death Doll." It was the doll of bad luck that one of the candidates had to carry on a night combat equipment parachute jump. They gave the doll to a candidate named Trammel. Trammel was a little guy who had endured more than his share of harassment because of his size. Sure enough, as soon as the doors to the plane opened Trammel's reserve parachute activated and started to snake towards the door. This was the worst possible scenario for a jumper in the airplane. If the parachute got out the door, the wind could catch it and violently extract the jumper and anything in his path from the airplane. Nearby Rangers dove on the parachute and saved Trammel from this fate. The legend of the death doll lived on.

Early one morning SSG Lowe loaded us onto a "cattle car" and we headed to the backside of Fort Benning for a week of field training. There we practiced patrolling, ambushes, and raids to learn the Standard Operating Procedures (SOPs). We would be expected to know how to execute these drills when we arrived at our assigned Ranger Battalion. This was also our first indoctrination into what it was like to be cold in Ranger style.

As soon as we arrived, it began to rain and the temperatures continued to drop throughout the day. Late in the afternoon snow flakes started to fall. Some of the cadre had been late and SSG Lowe wanted to move out and execute some counter-tracking measures to see if the other cadre could trail us. We moved by walking only in running streams and creek beds. If we crossed a road, each man walked in the same tracks to leave no clue as to how many men had passed.

With light snow in the air and soaked to the bone, we crossed chest deep creeks and moved like ghosts through the woods. The conditions were terrible. The men were frozen and shivering so hard that it was difficult to whisper. Believe it or not, we loved every minute of it!

That evening we moved into a perimeter for the night and made three-man buddy teams with which to rotate thirty-three percent security. At any one time at least one of the three had to be alert and pulling security duty. We were warned that the cadre would attempt to get into the perimeter during the night and take out the command post in the middle. The threat was simple. If they succeeded, we would pay in pain and sweat.

The night was bitter cold to our wet bodies and all we had was our poncho and poncho liners to stay warm. There was no such thing as a sleeping bag. For years I thought they were only issued in basic training. We used the one basic tool we had available to us to stay warm and used it well—pushups. I did not sleep one wink that night and if I didn't do a few thousand pushups I would be surprised. Regardless of our effort, we heard a loud explosion to our rear as an artillery simulator destroyed the command post. There was no reason to worry about staying warm anymore because we got the promised penalty for failure.

We started the Ranger Indoctrination Program with 124 candidates and graduated thirty-four. I graduated number two in my class behind a guy named Neil Reilly. Each of us had to recite a stanza of the Ranger Creed and the one who did it better would be the Honor Graduate. I botched it up and Neil got the prize.

This was the end of six months of continuous training that culminated with the opportunity to serve in the 75th Ranger Regiment. We had earned the right to wear the coveted black beret and basked in the moment. After graduation, nine of us loaded up for the ride over to the 3/75 Ranger Battalion compound, at the Harmony Church area of Fort Benning. Doug and I arrived on 22 February 1986.

# Chapter 2
## Black Chinook

The 75th Ranger Regiment was a Special Operations unit cloaked with secrecy and the subject of great rumor and speculation. The Ranger facilities were intimidating in themselves. Eight-foot, green plastic sealed, chain link fences topped with six strands of barbed wire surrounded the compound. A passerby could not see in and there ended the basic knowledge of the Ranger Regiment by those outside the green fence. Even the loved ones of the men in the unit did not know the entire scope of what went on within. In fact, many Rangers did not have the opportunity to see the "Big Picture."

Inside that fence resides the most professional, intense and lethal Light Infantry unit in the world. Rangers are characterized by bold and aggressive strike operations. It is a unit of volunteers who have proven themselves in pain and sweat and who live the ethos of the Ranger Creed.

### RANGER CREED

*Recognizing that I volunteered as a Ranger. Fully knowing the hazards of my chosen profession. I will always endeavor to uphold the prestige, honor and high Esprit de Corps of my Ranger Regiment.*

*Acknowledging the fact that a Ranger is a more elite soldier who arrives at the cutting edge of battle by land, sea or air. I accept the fact that as a Ranger my country expects me to move further, faster and to fight harder than any other soldier.*

19

*Never shall I fail my comrades. I will always keep myself mentally alert, physically strong and morally straight. I will shoulder more of the task, whatever it may be, one hundred percent and then some.*

*Gallantly will I show the world that I am a specially selected and well-trained soldier. My courtesy to superior officers, neatness of dress, and care of equipment shall set the example for others to follow.*

*Energetically will I meet the enemies of my country. I shall defeat them on the field of battle. For I am better trained and will fight with all my might. Surrender is not a Ranger word. I will never leave a fallen comrade to fall into the hands of the enemy and under no circumstances will I ever embarrass my country.*

*Readily will I display the intestinal fortitude required to fight on to the Ranger objective and complete the mission, though I be the lone survivor. Rangers lead the way!*

Army Rangers continuously conduct extremely difficult and dangerous training focused on the forecasted threats to national security. No unit in the army expends more live ammunition, has more state of the art equipment, trains in more environments around the world, or demands higher standards of performance from its soldiers. The Ranger Regiment is ready to deploy anywhere in the world within 18 hours, 365 days a year.

When I arrived at 3rd Ranger Battalion, I was assigned a room and then taken to meet my Platoon Sergeant, Sergeant First Class (SFC) Mark Keith. He was from the Georgia and Alabama area and had a smooth, confident, and likeable demeanor. He just smiled, asked me if I had any issues he may have to deal with, and then introduced me to my Forward Observer, Sergeant (SGT) Libby.

I would be SGT Libby's Radio and Telephone Operator (RTO). This job entailed being a pack mule to carry a radio, Laser Range Finder, binoculars, and Laser Target Designator. All of the equipment was required to complete our mission as a Forward Observer Team in the Special Operations community. It was SGT Libby's job to train me and keep me out of trouble.

A week later SGT Libby told me we would do a twelve-mile road march with all mission essential equipment. We had three Fire Support Teams of eight Rangers. Each eight Ranger team further broke down into three two-man Forward Observer teams and an added Fire Support Sergeant and a Fire Support Officer. Each team would start at a thirty minute interval and with the same exact packing list. It wasn't meant to be a competition, but it quickly dissolved into a race to see which team could get the fastest time.

When I put on my rucksack it weighed around 110lbs and cut into my shoulders. Military rucksacks were designed to get on and off quickly. All the weight was carried on your shoulders with no waist strap. I thought, *This is gonna suck!* Three hours later, I had endured the worst march of my life, yet I had proven I could 'ruck' (march with a rucksack) as well as the rest of the team and then some.

My reward was blistered feet and two terrible friction burns on the small of my back. Only someone who has had one of those burns can appreciate the pain of getting into the shower. I didn't know it at the time but for the next nine years I would compare every rucksack march and movement with that one and think, *This isn't so bad.*

The next major event was a Company jump into Fort Bragg, North Carolina to do an exercise with the Readiness Brigade of the 82nd Airborne Corps. We were to jump into a simulated airfield and secure it for the arrival of the 82nd. It was my first night mass tactical parachute jump in the Battalion and I was so nervous I had a stomach ache. Jumping in the Battalion is not anything like in Airborne School. Airborne School is a controlled and relatively low stress environment. A jump in the Ranger Battalion is all business and laced with intensity.

After a roller-coaster low-level approach of twenty minutes, which threatened to separate every soldier from the food in his stomach, we approached the drop zone. The doors opened and the rush of the wind drowned out the commands from the Jumpmaster. The plane was too crowded to get everyone hooked up. Rangers stood on the seats and on the floor to make room to reach the anchor line cable!

The Jumpmaster screamed, "Go!" The rear of the stick then pushed the entire row of jumpers toward the door to get everyone out as quickly as possible. The jumpers exited both doors at once and the night sky was filled with traffic.

We jumped, assembled and waited for the arrival of the 82nd. Captain (CPT) Krom, the Battalion Fire Support Officer, for whom I was the RTO said, "The Heavy Drop will be here in five minutes." I thought, *Heavy Drop? What's a Heavy Drop?* A few minutes later I heard a loud metallic crash echo through the night as a Sheridan tank crashed to the ground. I could just imagine being hurt on the drop zone and then being squashed by a tank. The next morning a C-130 transport plane landed on a dirt runway and flew us back to Fort Benning.

Road marching became an incredibly arduous affair that occurred far too often. The Rangers dreaded the road marches and it was said they never got easier. The pounding on your feet and legs took its toll and stress fractures were very common. You marched until you collapsed from heat exhaustion or completed the task. If you failed for any reason to arrive at the final destination ready to fight, you were considered to be weak-minded. Often, mock ambushes were utilized to ensure the unit was prepared to fight at any moment. You had to be alert and keep your head in the game.

Over time you learned to deal with the pain. The secret to the road march was the relationship of your mind over the pain of the moment. Often we joked, "Pain was a sign of weakness leaving the body." The NCOs kept an eye on their soldiers and moved up and down the ranks to ensure everyone kept pace.

*Doug and I at Fort Benning, Georgia.*

On a muggy morning we conducted a road march around the back side of Victory Pond. It was only about a six-mile march but the air was hot and heavy. After just a few minutes the sweat soaked our clothing and the conditions were right for the weak to fall out. At the four-mile point a young Ranger just ahead of me passed out and collapsed in a heap on the side of the road.

SSG Kelly walked up to the Ranger and began to kick and slap the guy to see if he was coherent. He said, "C'mon you weak mother fucker, wake up!" Another Ranger stopped and took the opportunity to urinate on the side of the road. While he conducted his business, he made a joke about trying to "cool off" the passed out Ranger. Yet another Ranger stopped and picked up the incoherent Ranger's weapon and the entire formation continued on without missing a beat.

As Rangers passed out from heat exhaustion a medic or a Ranger buddy would stick them with an IV to get fluid back into their bodies. A truck would trail the formation and then pick up all of the fallouts. They would be delivered to where we were headed or taken back to the Aid Station for medical treatment.

This may seem like a harsh mentality, but one has to understand this was a Spartan *man's* world and we were feeding off each other's energy. We were expected to perform, excel, and lead in a very strong and competitive environment. It was a unit of leaders – leaders leading future leaders. Competition and friction between junior Rangers was intense. During the stress of a road marches differences were often settled by hand to hand combat inside the wood line. The resultant ripped ear or gouged eye was always explained away as an accident.

Later that year, we executed a daytime twelve-mile road march on Viequez Island, Puerto Rico. Even though we came from the heat of Georgia the heat and humidity of Puerto Rico could be ruthless. The day prior we started to intake large amounts of water to pre-hydrate for the march. We had a guy in the platoon with a history of passing out. Therefore, to aid his hydration we administered two IV bags before we started.

The teams started at staggered intervals and we pushed through the morning to try and finish before the mid-day heat. At the six-mile point the heat was stifling and this Ranger collapsed. His eyes rolled back in his head and he began to have a seizure. A medic administered six IVs in an attempt to reduce his core temperature while a MEDEVAC helicopter was called from Roosevelt Roads Naval Station.

That Ranger had possible internal organ damage. Therefore, the decision was made to release him from the Battalion for his own good. He told his father in Alabama that he had been terminated unjustly and his father called his Congressman. The next thing you know, we had a Congressional Investigation at the Battalion wanting to know why this fine young man was being abused. In the end it was determined the soldier was given the proper care.

The intensity of the PT was no different than the road marching. Group PT was done five days a week and supposed to supply your body twenty percent of the training it needed. The remainder was to come from each individual's personal work ethic and on his own time.

One thing that will always be said about Army Rangers is that they can run! My team consistently ran six minute and fifteen second miles. Only two people could not keep the pace. It just so happened those two Rangers were our Team Leader, First Lieutenant (1LT) Ed Reinfurt, and Team Sergeant, SFC Jeff Hoff. They kept trying to throw odds and ends into the runs to get a break. Buddy carries, football style karaoke twists, and cross-country runs were thrown in much of the time. Their delay tactics were to no avail. The rest of us would complain the pace was too slow and this was a bunch of crap. Sooner or later the Lieutenant would give in and let us increase the pace to the finish.

Black Chinook

The first six months of these runs were no piece of cake. It generally took that long for a new Ranger's body to adjust to this type of running and we all suffered the initial pain. Some days you felt great, and on others you felt like crap. Either way it didn't matter because there would be a very aggressive NCO watching us like a hawk to make sure we gave every bit of effort. At the conclusion of the run, we could expect muscle-failure upper-body exercises and a barrage of other exercises until it made you sick. The individual Ranger's physical ability did not determine when the exercise session would end. It was the physical capacity of the NCO leading the PT that set the standard. His endurance had been expanded by training for months. As a new Ranger, those first few months of Physical Training were something to be feared. Any thought of socializing or having a few beers on a work night was a very bad idea. It could only result in increased pain the next morning at PT.

If an individual had the physical tools to complete the mission and was giving one-hundred percent of personal effort, he had nothing to worry about. If he was slacking he was like a piece of red meat to a vulture. I saw soldiers knocked into ditches and counseled as a "pogue" or for being "weak" countless times. *Pogue* was a term for someone not giving his all and having a weak mind. I was personally one of the worst in this area. I had no sympathy for the new Rangers. If some weak individual slowed my team down, it gave me an excuse to bite his head off and make him pay with PT runs in the evening.

In 1988, the 75th Ranger Regiment determined the run standards were out of control. The new legal run time would be eight minutes per mile plus or minus fifteen seconds. We were also required to have a measured course. This upset every man who could run well, and of course, the slow Rangers thought this was a great idea. A bit of Ranger ingenuity had the answer

26

for this small hindrance to training. We would sprint the first nine-tenths of a mile and then go back and pick up any fall-outs. If there were no fall-outs, we would just slow down and do pushups or crunches to ensure we did not cross that mile mark before eight minutes minus fifteen seconds.

The Ranger Battalions in the late 1980's were very hard both mentally and physically. No excuses were accepted for poor performance. Weak links amongst the ranks were not tolerated. Everyone understood the standard. It was the individual's job to meet or exceed them. Failure to achieve the standards after 90 days resulted in being shipped to another unit. Rangers came and went in large numbers. I remember making a list for my Platoon Sergeant of over fifty soldiers in the platoon who had been "terminated" in two years. Many left due to discipline problems, but most left because of injury. Stress fractures in the feet and legs were common along with assorted broken bones. If a Ranger got hurt, he had sixty days to be mission capable. Should an injury require a longer healing period, the Ranger would be shipped to another unit and provided an opportunity to again attend RIP at a later date. Almost every Ranger had the physical tools to succeed. They learned to tap that potential through tough and consistent training.

Early one morning I was standing in front of the Company Headquarters waiting to start PT when a soldier came running across the compound. He was in a hurry to accomplish something and stepped into a freshly dug posthole. His leg made a loud, "SNAP!" as the bone broke—talk about bad luck!

Luck was a huge factor and I had always been lucky. In 1987, my platoon executed a night iteration of a live-fire exercise on Cactus Whitson Range at Fort Benning. We assaulted the objective and occupied the "enemy's" foxholes to repel the expected enemy counter-attack. It was my job to call the 60mm mortar illumination round to signify the approaching enemy.

At the direction of the Platoon Sergeant, I called on my radio for the illumination round. It popped to our front and the light it provided revealed a series of target silhouettes. With identifiable targets we began to fire. The guy on my left was shooting an M-203 grenade launcher and the guy on my right an M-60 machine gun. The next thing I knew, the guy on my right had slumped to the bottom of the hole and the guy on my left had a look of shock on his face. I tapped the Platoon Sergeant on the shoulder (he was on the other side of the M-60) and pointed to the Ranger in the hole. He screamed, "CHECK FIRE!" the command was echoed down the line and the shooting slowly stopped.

The guy on my left had me reach under his flack vest. When I pulled my hand out, it was covered in blood. The guy on my right was unconscious and bleeding out the mouth from shrapnel in his jaw. It turned out a M-203 grenade had bounced off a tree and exploded right in front of my position. The man on my right and on my left both caught shrapnel and I was untouched in the middle. I was just lucky.

On another occasion in Puerto Rico, I was positioned with the support position on a Live Fire Exercise target. The two M-60 machine guns in the position were pouring steel down range at a series of bunkers located on a rise. There was a ravine between the knoll we were located on and the objective. The assault team moved up and assaulted through the wire. Once they were in the wire, the Company Commander, Captain (CPT) Thomas, and I moved to the right and intended to run under the rounds streaking over our heads.

I huffed about ten meters behind CPT Thomas while trying to keep up under the weight of my rucksack. Suddenly, we both stopped in our tracks and looked at each other. Right between us M-60 rounds were ripping through the grass. We paused for a second and quickly jumped into the ravine to get some cover. Apparently one of the guns was skipping rounds off a rock and the ricochets headed straight for the commander and me—lucky again.

Other Rangers weren't so lucky. Just before I arrived at 3/75 Ranger Battalion, a rifle Company had been conducting a fire and maneuver exercise at Cactus Whitson Range. A Ranger had crawled forward and was shot in the back of the head.

\*     \*     \*

In early 1986, the entire Regiment was alerted and directed to assemble at Hunter Army Airfield in Savannah, Georgia. As always, the call came in the middle of the night and the Ranger compound on Harmony Church was alive with activity. We packed our gear, palletized our equipment, and loaded buses. Then we conducted a covert ride down the deserted Sunshine Road on the back side of Fort Benning. We downloaded at the airfield and postured to load our aircraft. We took off from Lawson Army Airfield on a flight of C-141 Starlifter transport planes and soon landed at Hunter Army Airfield in Savannah.

As we landed, I saw Saber Hall for the first time. It was a star-shaped white building set atop a slight knoll and positioned on the end of the taxiways. The Regiment and a massive amount of rotary wing aircraft were present, spread out across the airfield. It was apparent this was no ordinary exercise. However, no official information was released. Within hours of arriving, the unofficial line said that the ammunition pallets were in the hangars and the Regiment was here to execute a real world mission. After the first command briefings, the situation was slowly briefed to key personnel. Apparently, a coup had overthrown the government of Surinam. Reports indicated two-hundred people were lined up alongside a river, beheaded, and the bodies thrown into the water. Large numbers of civilian refugees were fleeing into French Guiana and the Regiment had been assembled.

We rehearsed a raid into a small airstrip near our objective. The airstrip would be guarded by an enemy twin .50-caliber anti-aircraft gun. We would off-load and move toward a compound and surround the facility. Then we would broadcast on loud speakers, *"You are surrounded by U.S. Army Rangers.*

*Throw down your weapons and surrender or you will be killed!"* We conducted rehearsals and at certain times moved back into the hall to avoid passing Soviet satellites.

A full-dress rehearsal was executed a few nights before the expected mission. We loaded Special Operations helicopters fitted with long-range auxiliary fuel tanks and settled in for the long trip. As we flew, I peered out the partially opened ramp. There were helicopters as far as you could see against the night sky. It was an incredible sight. We flew a simulated flight route from Puerto Rico to French Guiana and executed the practice mission.

My bird actually broke down on the way and we returned to base, never completing our portion of the mission. As with every mission, there was a contingency plan and a cross-loading of key personnel across all the birds. This allowed the mission to be completed with or without us.

The next day, a huge weather front moved in with high winds and driving rain. We hunkered down, continued to rehearse and slogged around in mud up to our ankles. The storm lasted for three days. Somewhere during that time, the mission was scratched and the entire Regiment sent home. Nine years later, the "Old Timers" would still say, "Hey, do you remember "Operation Night Power" in 1986? That was a big one wasn't it?"

\*　　\*　　\*

**R**ANGER SCHOOL. In June of 1986, Sergeant (SGT) Libby asked me if I thought I was ready for Ranger School. I answered a bit forcefully to emphasize confidence, "Yes, Sergeant!"

SGT Libby eyed my reaction and asked, "Are you sure Private?"

I replied, "I'm sure Sergeant!" as I stood at parade rest.

He then leaned closer and said, "All right, you're going to the July Pre-Ranger Class. Get yourself ready." That was a big moment for any non-tabbed Ranger and I would be attending Ranger School as a Private First Class.

The next couple of weeks were a mixture of excitement and foreboding. I was happy as hell to get the chance to go but it was going to be a major challenge. I would attend Pre-Ranger for a month and then Ranger School for two more. Ranger School was known by all to be a serious "gut check" and sixty percent of the students who attended failed. To add a little pressure, everyone who attended from my platoon made it—everyone.

My pep talk by Staff Sergeant (SSG) Boyd, my Platoon Sergeant, was motivating: "When you go to Ranger School, don't even bother to think about quitting when the times get tough. If you quit, I will personally make your life a living hell. If you fail, you will have personally embarrassed me, your platoon, this Battalion, and our entire Ranger history. Besides, when you are freezing your ass off in the mountains and desert, we'll be sucking it up just as bad, or worse, than you are. So just remember its not better back home and we'll smoke your pussy ass if you quit. Got it?"

I had it, and I replied, "YES, SERGEANT!"

I arrived for Pre-Ranger in the same compound that the Ranger Indoctrination Program had been conducted in. We occupied the same barracks, got issued equipment and organized into platoons. The course was run exactly like Ranger School except it stressed Operations Orders. These were the written and verbal orders, in a structured format, which outlined our operations. The entire first week we learned to plan and deliver these orders.

We road marched, did hand to hand combat, huge amounts of physical training, obstacle courses, and land navigation. The hours were long and tedious but the information was invaluable. After the first two weeks, we moved to the Ranger training area near Weems Pond, on the east side of the post.

Once we arrived at the site, it was more land navigation and then straight to the planning bays. This was the bread and butter. We received our orders from higher headquarters and began our Squad and platoon Operations Order development. At first, it was slow and painful, but slowly we began to build speed and we improved steadily. Strangely enough, the two lessons I learned from the training had nothing to do with planning. They had to do with food.

This was the time I had my first LRRP ration. A LRRP ration is a bag of dehydrated food which Long Range Reconnaissance Patrols once carried because of their light weight. The bag held a dry powder to which you added water to make mush. The consistency reminded you of oatmeal with a meaty taste. It may not have tasted good but it did fill you up and that turned out to be the most important thing.

The other lesson dealt with a soldier's lifeblood—coffee. We could not build fires and did not have any heat tabs to heat the water, so I was extremely unhappy. I noticed two soldiers heating a cup of water a few yards away and went to investigate. They had taken a packet of peanut butter from their ration and squirted liquid insect repellent on it. They let it soak for a second and then lit it with a match. The repellent started to burn and sucked more fuel from the oil in the peanut butter and voilà—hot water.

Pre-Ranger culminated with a Field Training Exercise (FTX) to measure our competence with all that we had learned. Three days and nights we planned and executed numerous training missions. The focus was on the conduct of Ranger traditional missions. This included raids, ambushes, and recons, and we performed them time and time again.

After the final mission, we assembled around the instructors for the last time. A Ranger Cadre Sergeant who had come from the British Special Air Services (SAS) addressed the entire group. "Rangers, we have taught you all that you need to know to get through Ranger School. This is my advice to you to make things seem like they have a direction when you're tired, cold and hungry. You are gonna be gone for fifty-eight days. What gave me strength was to make believe I was fighting with a Ranger Battalion in a little war. That everyone around me was in the Battalion. You have to succeed for the Battalion. It worked for me."

\*     \*     \*

We had the weekend off and on Sunday afternoon, 28 August 1986, reported to the 4th Ranger Training Brigade on Fort Benning for Ranger School Class Number 13-86. In 1986, the school was still fifty-eight days long with no administrative breaks. The only breaks we would see for two months were two eight-hour breaks between certain phases. The phases at the time were: City Week and Benning Phase at Fort Benning; Mountain Phase at Dahlonega Georgia; Desert Phase at Dugway Proving Grounds, Utah; and finally Swamp Phase at Eglin Air Force Base, Florida.

The school sat just across a small piece of woods from the 3/75 Ranger Battalion compound at Harmony Church. We were met by the Ranger School cadre and from the time our feet hit the ground we ran everywhere and did more pushups than I can remember. It was the same simple philosophy—treat the candidates like crap and the weak will fall out. It worked and from the first day students began to disappear steadily.

When any Ranger was missing, we said he was picked up by the *Black Chinook*. It was a metaphor Rangers used to describe the black bird of death coming in to pick-up their body. The *Black Chinook* of death—removing your body from the battlefield—much like the Grim Reaper. It could also apply to their just being "gone" from the unit, no longer with us, death, injury, or anything else. This generated a survivor mentality and we all wanted to avoid the *Black Chinook*.

City Phase was one week of Physical Training, hand-to-hand combat, classes and then more classes. We slept two to three hours each night and our alarm clock was an artillery simulator thrown into the barracks. Ten minutes later we were shaved, our teeth brushed, in formation and heading for Physical Training.

Each candidate had to pass all of the physical requirements to be in the course during this phase. The Physical Training test, five-mile run, swim test, and obstacle course were the minimum physical requirements. If you did not pass each event you were given your ticket home. Many Ranger Candidates did not pass these minimum physical tests. Most failed because of a weak mind rather than a weak body. This was an intimidating environment, but the events were not hard. If you wanted that coveted black and gold Ranger Tab you could gut out any event. Some candidates just decided it was not worth the hassle of being physically and mentally harassed. Therefore, they used the physical tests as a face-saving ticket back home to their cozy bed. It wasn't the size of the man, but the size of his heart.

At the conclusion of City Week, we conducted a twelve-mile road march through the remote backwoods of Fort Benning and arrived at the location of Benning Phase, Camp Darby. The road march again took more than its share of casualties. The heat was stifling and cramps and blisters took their toll. I personally didn't have any problem and the "Bat Boys" drew strength from each other.

"Bat Boys" was the name given to the candidates from the Ranger Battalions. We were all as cocky as could be because we considered ourselves real Rangers and this was just a school. Of course, that meant we took our share of abuse for the cockiness but that feeling of belonging to something special energized our intestinal fortitude. The cadre purposely dispersed soldiers from the same units across the student Battalion. Therefore, we would rarely see each other during the course. Whenever our paths did cross we smiled and gave each other the big thumbs up. We knew we were special. Here we were, privates from the Ranger Battalions in a school with primarily Officers, NCOs, and candidates from other services.

There was another major fact to be considered: the Bat Boys rarely failed because failure was unacceptable.

Benning Phase was almost a duplicate of the Pre-Ranger course I had just finished. We learned techniques and SOPs that would carry us through the rest of the course. It was conducted at a slow pace and learning was the key. If you couldn't get the procedures down here, you were sure to suffer in the phases to follow. The hardships of the Benning Phase are not very memorable. I do remember spending long nights of patrolling through the heavy under brush of Georgia while executing training mission after training mission.

My first leadership position was Squad Leader and the mission was to conduct a reconnaissance of a rebel camp. I assumed the position after I had led the patrol as compass man for the first five kilometers. At one point, we were drifting downhill as we paralleled a ridgeline. Therefore, I made a sharp veer to the left and uphill. When we got to the top, the Ranger Instructor (RI) halted the patrol, came to the front, and asked me what the hell I was doing.

I explained that I thought if we got to the top of the ridgeline, we could parallel the road and surely run right into the objective. He thought I was bluffing and said, "OK, Ranger, now you're the Patrol Leader. Show me where you are on the map." The old Patrol Leader handed over the map and then melted into the night. What a pogue! He had the map all night and now I had to point at the map, with a blade of grass, to within two-hundred meters of our actual location.

I used my compass to determine the road to our front was running north and south. I then compared that to the map and found that almost the entire road actually ran east and west. Only one little stretch ran north and south. I pointed at the map with a blade of grass and said, "We're right here, Sergeant."

Reluctantly the RI said, "I agree, let's get moving. You've got a timeline to meet." I had dodged another bullet.

The rest of the mission went smoothly and we were extracted on two MH-60 Blackhawks at first light. Prior to the arrival of the helicopters the Senior Evaluator called each Patrol Leader over to give them their grade. I didn't think I had any chance of a passing grade because of a disagreement with the RI. Regardless, I wanted to put my best foot forward. I straightened up my uniform, blocked my cap, and made sure my face camouflage looked good. Then it was my turn to receive my counseling and grade for my leadership position. I walked briskly to the instructor, put the butt of my weapon on the ground, and snapped to Parade Rest.

The RI was a bit surprised. He looked at his grade book, scribbled something with his pen, and started to talk. "You know, I don't agree with how you ran your patrol, but you did accomplish your mission. I'm gonna give you a "Go" but I'm also gonna give you some advice. Don't be so cocky and keep your RI informed of what you're doing!"

I used that little ritual each time I went to get my grade and it worked like a charm. I finished the course with six *Go's* and two *No Go's*. I attribute half of the *Go's* directly to my attempt to report with the appearance and demeanor of a Ranger.

\*     \*     \*

We left Benning Phase and rode charter buses east of Atlanta to Dahlonega, Georgia. This was the home of the Mountain Ranger camp. The camp was nestled into a little valley just south of the Tennessee Valley Divide. A beautiful spot if you were on a vacation. It was a terrible place if you were attending Ranger School. Our Squads occupied one of about ten old green cabins. These cabins had been used since the first Ranger school class and were little time capsules of the classes that had preceded us. There were hundreds of inscriptions from years past on the walls and rafters and the place had an incredible feeling of nostalgia.

The Mountain Phase would be broken into two sub-phases, Mountaineering and Patrolling. For two weeks we learned rope knots, mountaineering skills and actual rock climbing techniques. Rope bridges, rappelling, prussic climbing and evacuation of casualties were all instructed in depth.

The best part of this phase was that we got plenty of good food and sleep. Since it was hazardous to be hanging from the cliffs and ropes strung across the gullies, the instructors wanted everyone to be well rested and feeling strong. Therefore, it was undoubtedly the best phase of the course.

We would rise early and run to the chow line. Mmm— blueberry pancakes, bacon, sausage and eggs. We would eat until we were sick and then run back to the cabin. Because of the fresh air, it was the best food I had ever tasted. Of course, the fact that I was cinching my belt tighter and tighter, regardless of how much food I ate, had something to do with it. All good things had to come to an end, and the Mountaineering sub-phase was soon just a memory.

We moved to the planning bays and received our first missions. Our first patrol was a reconnaissance mission which would take us directly over the Tennessee Valley Divide (TVD) and on to Greasy Mountain—just another in an endless supply of painful mountains to trek.

We moved out from the camp and instantly the terrain started to get very steep. The time we had spent in Mountaineering sub-phase had seemed like a blessing but in reality had allowed our legs to lose their conditioning. Now our quadriceps screamed from moving uphill under the weight of our equipment. Up, up and up we went, but a lesson of the mountains was soon learned. No matter how far you went up, you were still going to go up some more.

There were a limitless number of lessons you were forced to learn the hard way. I formed a list of seven tenets that I followed on every patrol. First, never go over a major terrain feature but go around. It may be a longer distance, but you'll save time and a lot of energy. Second, make use of the logging trails that run around the hills. It may seem untactical, but you'll move quieter and faster. Also, by placing security forward of your patrol, you'll be safer than trudging through the brush. Third, the first man in your patrol has to be an experienced compass man. No other system works correctly. Fourth, always use two pace men and always stop four-hundred meters from your objective. Not two-hundred or you will certainly bump into it. Fifth, rotate the heavy rucksacks and key planning responsibilities or you'll burn out your best people. Sixth, if you have a break in contact (your patrol gets separated), stop the front half and DO NOT move. Send two men on a back azimuth, in the direction from which you just came, to find the back half. Seventh, after you start moving after any kind of halt, move about one-hundred meters, then stop to make sure you have everyone. Chances are someone fell asleep or is so delirious he is trying to put fifty cents into a tree to get a can of Coke. Each of these tenets was learned from experience.

The mountains began to take their toll in energy and injuries. We stayed awake for a minimum of twenty-two hours each day and continuously marched up and down those damned mountains. It was at this point that I realized my senses were getting especially keen. We were so hungry that our sense of smell was amazing.

One night we had stopped in a defensive perimeter. It was so dark you couldn't see your hand in front of your face. Suddenly, I caught a whiff of something in the breeze. I stood up and just followed my nose about twenty yards to the source. A soldier was sneaking a snack and had opened a cherry nut cake from his meal ration. The nut cake is the equivalent of a cookie and I had sniffed it twenty yards downwind, then followed it right to the package. I whispered into the darkness, "Gimme a bite." He had no choice but to comply because he was not supposed to be eating.

Each member of a Squad had a special talent that made him valuable to the group. Skills like land navigation, planning, staying awake, needing little food, and being able to carry extra weight. These individual strengths gave each man a special role to play. Any candidate who did not have a talent to contribute to the Squad was in danger at the end of each phase.

The last graded event of each phase was the student Peer Evaluations. Each student anonymously graded his peers numerically from top to bottom; the man with the highest number was the worst in the squad. The sum of the evaluations was averaged out to determine the man with the highest total score. If you were the high score, you had been "peered." Those candidates were either recycled or dropped from the course.

We made it through three grueling weeks in the mountains and arrived at our first Peer Evaluation. After the points were compiled the Battalion was formed. The Senior RI then read the names of the students that would not be going with us to the desert. One by one the names were called out, and every Ranger candidate held his breath. If your name was called, you stepped backward out of the formation and moved to the rear. In the end, a separate formation of about thirty candidates had formed and they stayed in the Mountain Phase. Some were recycled and some were dropped from the course. The rest of us did not have time to worry about that because we were headed to the deserts of Utah.

\*      \*      \*

The chartered commercial 727 airplane landed on a remote runway and unloaded us at Dugway Proving Grounds, Utah. It was a dark cloudy day with a cold wind blowing across the desert floor. We unloaded our gear and immediately received a mission to be executed that night. We had to plan, prepare our equipment, and then conduct a parachute jump just after dark.

I did not know it at the time, but that jump would turn out to be one of the worst of my career. A combination of cold thin air and a heavy rucksack caused me to hit the desert floor extremely hard. The wind blew me backward and I hit feet, butt, and then head. I was knocked out for an unknown amount of time. When I got my head together, I packed my gear and looked in all directions for the assembly aid used to draw all jumpers, from across the drop zone, to one location. That night it was supposed to be two amber lights. I looked all around me, saw two amber lights, and started to walk toward them. I had taken an azimuth with my compass and a half hour later those lights weren't getting any closer. It turned out I had been walking towards two security lights around a shed in the middle of nowhere. I did a 180-degree turn and headed back the other direction.

When I returned to the drop zone, the entire Battalion was on line looking for me. I materialized out of the darkness, and they were elated to find me. I explained to the RI that I had been knocked out and then headed in the wrong direction toward the security lights. He was so happy to see me that he didn't care where I had been and called a medic to check me out.

The medic decided I was fit to fight, and we moved out on our mission. It was soon apparent that I was not all right and had suffered a mild concussion. As we moved across the desert,

*Black Chinook*

I would just start to wander away from the patrol in a daze. I couldn't turn myself into the medic or I would be recycled. My Squad took care of me and assigned two men the mission of making sure I didn't wander away during the night. Unfortunately, about an hour later I got a Squad Leader position. My head was in such a daze that my Squad planned the mission for me. As I briefed this plan to the RI, my words were slurred and key points missed. The mission was a failure and I received a justified *No Go*. I dropped to four *Go's* and one *No Go*, but my main goal was a success. I bought myself some time to heal and did not get dropped from the course.

The desert had a whole new list of challenges and small pleasures. We would make grueling climbs on the mountains around Dugway, and when we reached the top the view was spectacular. On one such patrol, we reached the summit of a mountain just after dark and you could see the lights of Salt Lake City sparkling in the distance. It was beautiful. Then we climbed all the way to the desert floor and made a secured perimeter for the night.

The wind picked up and a light snow began to blow through the Spruce trees. Conditions were frigid and our hands and feet were aching with cold. Each man paired with his Ranger buddy and curled up under the same poncho and poncho liner—spooning like a husband and wife. Under these conditions no one cared about anything but staying warm.

Throughout our stay in the desert, a man could be cold and then hot, one second to the next. When we were stopped, we would put on extra layers of clothes to avoid the chill. Then these layers had to be removed before moving again. If you didn't remove them, you would break into a sweat within minutes and roast until the next stop. If you did take layers off in preparation for a move, you would freeze for twenty minutes until you exerted enough energy to get warm again. Every

44

Ranger in a patrol conducted changes of clothes only when directed to by the Patrol Leader. If you did it at your leisure, you would risk the security of the patrol and disrupt the smooth movement from one location to the next. Everyone grew accustomed to the system, but no matter what, when you stopped after sweating on a movement, the desert wind would chill you to the bone.

The desert was the first phase where the students had to balance mission completion with personal preservation. We had all lost twenty to twenty-five pounds of body weight and our stamina and strength had gone with it. Simple physical tasks became difficult and care had to be taken to spread the tasks across the platoon. Combined with extremely cold and dry conditions, our bodies were under a lot of stress; it was hard to stay warm and it was very hard just to eat. We would eat our one and a half meals a day and the food would just disappear. It wasn't uncommon to go a week without a bowel movement. Regardless of how much water one drank, the body was continually dehydrated and water was all that passed through. On that tenth day when the bowels did move, it had to be a close simulation of giving birth. Our bodies were going through hell.

For two weeks, we continuously marched across the desert, day and night, executing mission after mission. If a Ranger student could get two hours of sleep a day, he was doing well for himself. The rest of the time was spent planning or walking. Strangely enough, by this time we had learned to doze while standing and under extreme conditions, when we were moving. The body adapted to find little windows of rest by just drifting off a few moments at a time.

The last patrol ended at a civilian plane on a remote airstrip waiting to take us to the Swamp Phase in Florida. Again, we stood in formation and the names were called out for those who would not be moving on. A sizable platoon had fallen out and the command was then given for the remainder of us to load the plane. I always thought of those guys as casualties. You worked and supported each other the best you could, but in the end some guys were just gone. What could you do? You had to "Charlie Mike"—continue the mission.

I took my boots off on the plane to let my feet get some air during the flight. A few minutes later I was fast asleep. I awoke when the stewardess told me to fasten my seat belt for landing. Right away I tried to put on my boots. I couldn't get my feet in them! My hands and feet had swelled up during the flight. I pulled, stomped and finally jammed my feet into the boots. They would remain swollen for the next two days.

\*　　\*　　\*

The swamps of Florida were our last phase. We would simulate a fight against a guerrilla force in a Latin American country. The leader was named Julio and we would be attacking his bases and communications as we attempted to capture him and his equipment.

To graduate, each student needed a fifty percent *Go* rate on his leadership positions and a Platoon Leader position *Go*. I came out of the desert with a five *Go* and one *No Go* rate. All I had to do was stay healthy, get a Platoon Leader position *Go*, and stay motivated. The threat of being peered was always present.

On the first night I was given my Platoon Leader position for a reconnaissance mission. That night we moved through the swampy, wet, and extremely thick vegetation of Eglin Air Force Base. Then successfully located and reconnoitered the guerrilla outpost as directed. The next morning I had the *Go* I needed to meet all the requirements. Now I just needed to help my Ranger buddies earn the *Go's* they needed and survive the last Peer Evaluation.

It never stopped raining for our first week in Florida and the rain just rolled in like a wave. You could hear the falling water as it rumbled in the distance and moved closer. The rumble grew louder and louder until you were standing in a deluge. On many occasions, the lightening was so close we dropped our gear and weapons and got away from their metal components. We moved around the woods as lightening flashed and deafening thunder clapped very near us. We attempted any little maneuver to reduce the possibility of being struck. As a result of the rains, we were constantly wet and there was no way to get dry. We did not wear rain gear and were consistently up to our thighs in swamp water. To make matters worse, the rain finally subsided only to be replaced by a cold front. Now we were constantly wet and freezing cold. It was a continuous battle to try and stay warm and dry for any period at all.

At the beginning of the Florida Phase, we had picked up two recycles from the previous class. One was a Nigerian and the other was a Staff Sergeant from the 82nd Airborne. Both were totally starved, emaciated, and physically spent. Their depleted condition made them extremely susceptible to bouts of hypothermia day after day. We felt sorry for these guys and wanted them to make it through the course. When they collapsed, we actually took turns carrying them on our backs.

The Staff Sergeant showed me his driver's license and I was shocked. The picture showed a young, husky, and strong man who looked nothing like the man in front of me. This guy had been through hell and was being recycled again. He attempted to befriend me but he was in an impossible situation. Due to his condition he could not contribute to the team effort. Therefore, the only way he could survive the final Peer Evaluation was if we voted out one of our core team.

The Nigerian would be kept in the class and did not count against our peer evaluations. All Ranger candidates understood that students from allied forces were assured of passing the course. It was rumored that a foreign student had failed the course and upon returning to his home was beheaded for embarrassing his country. The Ranger Training Brigade and Army Infantry School must have determined this wasn't good for international relations.

The Nigerian officer had a Ranger Buddy named Toliver, from the 7th Infantry Division at Fort Ord, California. It was Toliver's job to keep an eye on him. It became comical because in the quiet and black of night you would hear, "Toleever, heelp Me! Toleever heelp Me!" and we would have to start lugging the guy through the forest again. In spite of our efforts, the combination of weather and cold finally got them both and the *Black Chinook* removed them from the field.

Florida was a tough phase but the end was in sight and that made it bearable. We conducted boat movements, boat insertions from Navy landing craft, airborne jumps, and air assault raids. We conducted mission after mission through the Florida swamps trying to catch the elusive rebel commander named Julio.

The final mission was a raid onto Julio's island to take out his largest base and command center. We would move offshore on the Navy LCM's (troop carriers like those used on D-Day) and then paddle quietly to shore in Zodiac assault boats. Once ashore, we would put four M-60 machine guns on a sand dune and then assault the objective in a textbook raid.

Earlier in the course, during a boat movement down the Yellow River, I had caught a RI's eye. We were having trouble getting our boats out of the water and some Rangers were being a bit lazy. I had gotten frustrated and irritated and physically motivated a few droning Rangers. The RI liked that and had given me a positive spot report. There must have been some cadre competition for this mission. Therefore, he wanted to make sure the M-60's in the support position did their job. As he assigned leadership positions for the night, he asked for me by name and put me in charge of the weapons Squad. A bit later he took me to the side and said, "Ranger, if you fail me, I'll make sure you don't graduate this course." This was the last night, I didn't need a graded position to graduate and now I was in the hot seat again!

During the planning of the mission, I left my Squad on the beach and went to help with the terrain model rehearsal. When I came back, my Squad had built a fire on the beach and the RI gave me an immediate *No Go* for losing control of my men. The mission had not even started and I had a *No Go*! To make matters worse, the RI told me that I was staying in the Leadership Position and if those guns didn't "talk" he would personally recycle me.

We infiltrated onto the beach and my crew low-crawled up and onto the berm. I estimated we were about two-hundred yards from the objective. It was my butt on the line and I was being a real asshole with my men. On a time hack, we opened fire with all four guns intending to rotate bursts from each weapon to keep up a continuous volume of fire. That way even if a gun jammed there would be a continuous noise to replicate no lull in firing. Two guns jammed after the first burst and the other two hummed for about a minute. As one gun jammed another, one would just get back into operation and begin firing. We completed our job in an ugly manner.

Julios' base was wiped out, but he wasn't there. A report came in over the radio that Julio had been spotted on the main land so we ran to the Zodiacs and paddled all the way across the sound to the mainland. Once onshore, we issued a Fragmentation Order (FRAGO). The platoons then moved out in different directions to try to catch Julio.

My platoon had to move three miles through the woodlands, cross the Yellow River and then set up an ambush on a road upon which Julio was expected to travel. When we reached the river, we determined we could walk across. The water came up to our armpits and there was no need for the rope bridge. I was about the fourth Ranger in the file. As each man in front of me stepped into the frigid water, you could hear him take a deep breath of pain and surprise as the cold water reached his groin. I turned around and whispered to the Ranger behind me, "Man, this is gonna suck!" After the last man crossed the river, we moved about fifty feet and a guy collapsed from hypothermia. We quickly carried him to the road and a vehicle came and took him out. I never saw him again and don't know if he ever graduated. This was the last night!

We got into position and just after daylight Julio came walking down the road with two other guys. Since we had to capture Julio alive, we shot the guys with him and Julio took off running down the road. We ran after him but we were so physically depleted that we couldn't catch up. Julio realized what was happening and slowed down so we could catch him.

That was it! The end of the course! No more starving, freezing, walking around like a zombie, or living with that incredible paranoia that something might happen to keep you from graduating. I received my promised *No Go* but it didn't matter. I finished the course with six *Go's* and two *No Go's*. Not bad for a Private First Class.

The Ranger graduation ceremony is a big event and a large crowd of family and friends gathered to celebrate with their new Rangers. It wasn't as big a day for the Bat Boys because this was an expected outcome of the school and it was understood that we were going "back to work." The crowning moment was the pinning on of the black and gold Ranger Tab that we had been chasing for the last three months. The cadre put on a great show with an explosion followed by Rangers executing an Australian rappel down a wall while firing M-60 machine guns. It was a great day.

I often think back to Ranger School and the lessons learned there. I remember having an extremely bad taste in my mouth for the way the course had been run. So many good soldiers had failed. So many poor soldiers had made it. A lot depended on the Squad you had been assigned to and your ability to function within that small group of men. If you were unlucky enough to fall into a Squad with small cliques, chances were you would have a rough time during the peer evaluations.

The worst stories of this came during the summer classes when large numbers of Officers from regular units and Officer Candidates from West Point and ROTC attended Ranger School. It was felt that if you were unlucky enough to be an enlisted soldier in a Squad heavy with officers you were finished. Many stories of the lower enlisted being "peered" by the officers sticking together filtered out each year. I personally had a balanced Squad and we had no cliques and no problems. We worked well as a team.

The final day we had "peered" a Staff Sergeant for being lazy. He had held his own but on the final day he was peered and dropped from the course. He was almost in tears and came to each of us and asked why. Before the vote our Squad made a pact to vote independently. We had just ranked him against the others and he had come out low enough on each of our cards to make him the overall last place. He was done because there was no recycle option after the final peer evaluation.

Ranger School was and is supposed to be a leadership school. I remember it as a survival school. We had to survive the cadre, lack of food, sleep, peer evaluations, the grading system, and the threat of injury. Ranger School had required a lot of luck and determination to succeed. I remember feeling that if it was a leadership school then an increase in food and sleep would surely create an environment that would promote learning. The other side of the coin would say those same stresses created an environment that brought out the best and worst from each individual. These brutal conditions made each candidate look inside himself and assess his own weaknesses and strengths.

I said goodbye to my buddies then headed back to the unit to find something to eat and enjoy a little time off. I had graduated on a Friday and walked through the woods back to the Battalion. After I dropped my gear in my barracks room, I went to the Fire Support office to see my Platoon Sergeant. SSG Boyd told me to take the weekend to pack my bags and be ready for duty on Monday. In contrast the infantry graduates got the next week off to rest.

I took my first opportunity to call home and tell my folks I had graduated and received my Ranger Tab. They were very happy and glad to hear from me. My mom said she would make my favorite of German chocolate cake with fudge frosting and send it through the mail. For now, I was headed to the Dolly Madison Bakery outlet on Victory Drive for donuts—lots of donuts.

# Chapter 3
## Ranger Training

Ⅰn 1988, the 3/75 Ranger Battalion made a trip to the Jungle Operations Training Center (JOTC) at Fort Sherman, Panama. The focus would be to work on our small unit counter-insurgency operations. It would be a progressive training schedule tailored to a curriculum dictated by the Battalion. The remainder of the standard course was discarded.

*SGT Leonard Jones and me making a hootch.*

Fort Sherman, Panama, had numerous old gun emplacements and magazines. These consisted of concrete pads where coastal defense guns used to be positioned to protect the canal up through World War II. These positions made excellent locations for training sites and the Opposing Forces (OPFOR) were placed there to be used as targets.

The training started with classes on guerrilla warfare, mines and booby traps, navigation, waterborne operations, plants and animals, and live fire ranges. The live fire operations began with Squad level exercises and progressed through platoon level maneuvers. At the end of the first week the training changed to raids and ambushes in a jungle environment.

The first week was nothing but quality training and becoming acclimatized to the lush tropical environment. This exhilarating climate mixed with swims in the lagoon, physical training, and evening Corona beer made it seem like paradise. We trained and trained hard but the tropical atmosphere injected you with energy!

The second week was the beginning of raid operations with our attached Special Operations aviation unit. We conducted refresher fast rope training and loading and unloading of the aircraft. We then began a series of platoon and Company sized raids on objectives around the post. I remember being packed into a UH-60 Blackhawk and flying a nap of the earth flight route which skimmed the dense canopy of the jungle. The chopper then dropped off the edge of the canopy to just above the surface of the Tigris River. We then flew up the river, just above the water, with a dark and ominous jungle on both sides. From there we veered back up and over the canopy and in towards the target. The nose of our bird rose momentarily as we quickly decelerated and sank into a hole in the jungle canopy. Our wheels hit the ground and we "unassed" the bird with adrenaline pumping. That would be the norm for operations in Panama—big helicopters in very small clearings in the jungle canopy.

This trip to the jungle would turn out to be very expensive on the manpower of the 3rd Ranger Battalion. All training is dangerous and has its risks but the jungle offered new and unforeseeable threats. The nights were pitch black under the triple canopy jungle. On one night a Company assumed a defensive perimeter to wait for morning. Sometime before morning, a *Widow Maker* (old rotted tree ready to fall) crashed to the ground on top of three Rangers manning the perimeter. It was a freak accident and the result was terrible—one Ranger dead, one with internal organ damage, and one with broken limbs.

A few days later, a Ranger on a live-fire exercise opened his jammed M60 machine gun. When the cold air hit the red hot round lodged inside the chamber it caused a "cook off." The live round exploded and the shell casing blew backwards out the open feed tray and through the gunner's calf.

On that same day, I was laying in the grass between a guy named Specialist (SP4) Jackson on my left and Captain (CPT) Cronin on my right. CPT Cronin yelled, "I've been bit!" I thought he was joking and glanced over expecting to see him laughing. I replied, "Yeah, right!" He then jumped up and started stomping around the area in disbelief. First Sergeant McDuffie, who was nearby did not like snakes and left little dust clouds where his feet used to be as he rocketed to a small road nearby. SP4 Jackson and I kicked around in the grass until we found the snake. Jackson then stomped on its head to kill it. We identified the dead snake as a little Fer-de-lance; an extremely poisonous and territorial viper. We had invaded his turf and he had bitten the Captain. A Fer-de-lance bite was usually fatal unless the bitten limb was amputated. CPT Cronin's bite could be even more lethal because this was a baby snake. The young snakes typically had not learned to regulate the amount of venom it released into a bite wound. This had the makings of a very bad situation.

A MEDEVAC helicopter landed and then whisked CPT Cronin, and the snake, to the hospital. When he landed, he was greeted by a priest who read him his last rites. The doctors explained that a woman had been there the previous week and died because she would not allow them amputate her bitten limb. When CPT Cronin got back to the unit, he explained that he had "crapped his pants." All the talk of last rites and amputated limbs were not giving much hope to the situation. After inspection of the wound, the doctors determined he was lucky. The snake's fangs had not gotten all the way through the skin. No meat cutting was necessary to amputate the limb.

The Jungle Operations Training Center had offered its own set of challenges and training opportunities and we had done well. It wasn't uncommon at all for us to be heading home having lost another comrade. As we loaded the airplanes it seemed routine.

*     *     *

My first Battalion sized mission was a deployment to the Joint Readiness Training Center (JRTC), at Fort Chaffee, Arkansas. The JRTC is the Army's Light Infantry evaluation center. This was the site where all light infantry units would go once a year to evaluate the readiness of their procedures, soldiers, and staff. The basis for evaluation was Army Doctrine and therein was the problem. The center had regular army evaluators trying to evaluate Special Operations Forces against conventional doctrine. Also, the center was famous for its unrealistic training scenarios and the

Opposing Forces (OPFOR) always had the advantage. Officially, the Cadre at the center would go out of its way to ensure everything was "on a level playing field." My experience provided firsthand evidence to the contrary.

Preparations for the initial mission began in the Ranger compound at Fort Benning. The Battalion was to conduct an Airborne Operation into Arrowhead Drop Zone on Fort Chaffee. Then move on foot to attack an enemy compound six miles away. The objective was to secure American hostages being held by a hostile country. We conducted the jump, secured the airfield in short order, and moved to the compound with the hostages. Two Companies would assault the compound and secure the "precious cargo" (hostages). The remaining Company would block the avenue of approach against any enemy reinforcements.

As two Ranger Companies approached the wire around the compound all hell broke loose. The initial breach teams were casualties in short order. Continued attempts to breach the wire with wire cutters were repelled. Smoke billowed to obscure the attacking Rangers in the wire, but wave after wave were repelled.

As this was happening, a four Ranger Fire Team slipped into the compound from the rear and reached the building with the POW's. On the outside of the building, the team assumed the basic room clearing stack. After entering the doorway each member of the team had a sector of responsibility to focus and engage any enemy. The team then burst into the room to secure the hostages. The problem was the guards were in sandbag bunkers inside the building. They killed the entire team seconds after it entered the building. The mission was a failure and the two Ranger Companies destroyed. The Battalion broke contact and withdrew into the woods.

After that mission the Battalion Commander said, "The gloves are off!" and we took the fight to the OPFOR in Ranger style. We set up ambushes on all the roads and bridges and paralyzed the OPFOR's ability to move his forces. They moved and we killed them—then disappeared quickly into the woods. It was too easy because the OPFOR was lazy. They would not pursue us into the swamps or creek bottoms and we could move about as we pleased.

The final mission was an air assault raid directly onto a remote compound to rescue those same hostages. The OPFOR was frustrated at not being able to find us on the countryside and threatened to kill the hostages to draw us out into the open. The plan called for one Company to infiltrate by foot and two companies to be flown by Special Operations aircraft directly over the compound. The Company on the ground would open fire as a diversion. The two from the air would Fast Rope inside the compound's defenses.

I would be with the Company that would infiltrate on foot and establish an overwatch position on a hill above the compound. From there we would call in fires to take out enemy anti-aircraft positions. Through the night we marched single file over the razorback ridges of Arkansas. Laden with equipment we climbed near vertical ridges to reach the summit. After about twenty steps across the narrow ridgeline we would start down the near vertical opposite side. About two hours before daylight we found ourselves on another near vertical cliff. We would have to remain there until the next evening. Having decided there was little chance of being discovered on the cliff face we camouflaged our position as best we could. Then we posted security and pulled out our small Gortex sleeping bags.

This was actually the first time since basic training that I had used a sleeping bag. It was the issue of the first Gortex sleeping bag that could be cinched into a small ball and therefore not take up much space in the rucksack. We then tied the strings of the bags to small trees on the incline. We slept throughout the day hanging like giant cocoons.

The raid that was coming that evening would be recorded by NBC News with night filming equipment and shown as a special feature. The news reels showed the four CH-47 Special Operations aircraft hover over the compound with smoke grenades raining out the doors. The ropes came out, followed by Rangers pouring down the ropes. Once inside the compound they disappeared into the smoke. The OPFOR was shocked by the noise and smoke and the defenses were neutralized quickly.

The hostages were again held in a metal type pole shed with the bunkers on the inside. We had learned our lesson on the first objective and had come prepared. A huge Ranger named SGT Lambatina fired up a Special Operations gas-powered metal saw and quickly sawed a square hole into the side of the building. Sparks rained onto the shocked defenders and the film crew picked up the deafening sound of metal cutting metal followed by Rangers pouring through the hole. They killed the guards, rescued the hostages, and moved the "precious cargo" to the extraction site.

The final days at JRTC ended with a visit by the Honorable John O. Marsh, the Secretary of the Army. The Battalion was dressed in full combat equipment and stood in formation as he was led through the ranks. The rotation had been a success and as always many lessons had been learned.

\*     \*     \*

On a Saturday morning in 1987, I was walking across the almost deserted compound when I heard CPT Cullinane, the Company Commander, yell my name. "Specialist Combs, do you want to go to Jumpmaster School?"

I yelled back, "You have to be a Sergeant to go to that school, Sir."

"No, just a Corporal and you are promoted effective immediately. Get some rank and be in Jumpmaster School Monday at 0600!"

I was stunned—Jumpmaster School was not an easy course. It was a high-pressure school teaching the proper rigging and inspection of an airborne paratrooper and his equipment, preparation of the aircraft, the briefing of the flight crew, actions in the aircraft, spotting the drop zone, and putting the jumpers out the door. You also were trained to perform duties as the Drop Zone Safety Officer (DZSO). The DZSO set up the drop zone, measured the winds, estimated the drift of the jumpers, put out panels to mark the drop zone, and then talked the airplane over the computed release point. If anything went wrong, the DZSO was directly culpable.

A Mobile Training Team (MTT) was coming from Ft Bragg to train Ranger Jumpmasters. The next two weeks were a mind-numbing dose of studying nomenclatures, procedures, and inspecting hundreds of jumpers prior to testing. It was the same old thing—the paranoia of failure. All of us worked our butts off to ensure we succeeded.

First Lieutenant (1LT) Snukis was a Charlie Company Platoon Leader attending the course. 1LT Snukis was about five-feet and ten inches tall but very thick with no neck and a big chest and arms. During the course he was having a bit of trouble with the Jumpmaster Inspections. He was basically throwing around the soldiers he was inspecting as he tried to get faster and faster. When the Jumpmaster found a "gig," he was required to announce it in the perfect nomenclature which was a bit of a tongue twister. Every time 1LT Snukis got it wrong, he would become so frustrated his head turned red. Then he would have to stomp away, cuss some expletives, and try and shake it off.

I had no problem with the testing but many of the candidates had to retest under extreme pressure. After the testing, it was time to put jumpers out of the aircraft. Each candidate put out two sticks of jumpers and executed actions in the aircraft before completing all requirements.

The course was difficult, and considering I was only a new corporal, I was pleased with my performance. This was my first chance to evaluate myself against my peers in a purely Ranger course. I felt confident in my abilities and the result was my qualification as a static line Jumpmaster and the awarding of my Senior Parachutist Wings.

\* \* \*

Two years later that terrible thought of falling off the handles of the "Slide for Life" would finally be confirmed. SSG Dave Gibbs had fallen from the Slide for Life. He had been training for the "Best Ranger Competition" and practicing running the entire water confidence course for speed. When Dave reached the "Slide for Life," he climbed to the top of the forty-foot tower, grabbed the handles from the Safety NCO, and stepped off the platform. He went about six feet down the cable and stopped.

It turns out the Safety NCO had forgotten to unhook the pulley from the safety rope attached to the top of the tower. Dave went down the cable to the end of the rope and then just stopped. He held on and tried to get a leg up to hook the cable but his hands were slippery from the previous events. The Safety tried to pull him back by hand but couldn't because of the weight. He also didn't have a knife to cut the pulley free. Dave hung there until he lost his grip and fell to the ground forty feet below.

I was at the Battalion when Guy Fichtelman came to tell us what happened. We jumped in my Trans Am and raced to Martin Army Hospital where Dave had been taken. On the way Guy recounted how he had seen Dave fall and disappear behind some brush. He said you could see sticks and leaves fly into the air when he hit. They ran to the spot and Dave was still alive but "fucked up."

We finally arrived at the emergency room and went behind the curtain where Dave was being worked on. He was lying there on a table and he looked bad. I walked in and he greeted me with the calmest voice, "Hey Dave, how ya doing?"

I answered back, "How are YOU doing?"

We started talking and he recounted what had happened to him. I could hear the frustration in his voice as he relived looking down to find out he was still over land. There was also a concrete retaining wall along the water. Dave tried to find a spot to land which would give him a chance. He fell and missed the concrete and luckily hit some small pine trees and brush which helped to break his fall. The result was a fractured pelvis and broken leg. Dave was fortunate to recover and went on to have a great career as a Drill Sergeant and later in Special Forces.

\*       \*       \*

O ur Fire Support Platoon had been reorganized to provide support of the infantry Companies within the Battalion. Alpha Team would support A-Company and B and C Teams would support their corresponding Companies. This meant we had to be prepared to provide infiltration teams that could call for fire support assets to support any mission in air, water, or overland insertion operations. To fulfill this requirement we started sending our Rangers to Special Skills schools such as Military Free Fall School, Scuba School, Naval Gunfire School, Joint Firepower Control Course, Pathfinder School, and others.

Since I had completed my Static Line Jumpmaster requirement, I was earmarked to complete the Military Free Fall School. From there I would become a Military Free Fall Jumpmaster. This was an ambitious plan because attendance at these schools had to be balanced with our normal Ranger training and mission cycles. It was also a bit of a nervous time because it was somewhat understood that if you were at a school when the "balloon went up" you could be left behind.

I arrived at the John F. Kennedy Special Warfare Center, located at Fort Bragg, and checked in with the student Staff Duty Officer. Each of us was assigned a room for the next month and settled in to wait for the first day of class.

The classroom instruction hit a wide range of topics. Emphasis was placed on aircraft procedures, how to move your body to fly in the air, exiting the aircraft, and jump commands. We also learned to pack our own parachute rigs. In static line jumps, you had the luxury and confidence of knowing a professional parachute rigger had packed your parachute. Now we would only jump a chute we had personally packed. The first week moved hard and fast and soon we were loaded on an airplane and taken to the wind tunnel.

At the time, Wright Patterson Air Force Base, Ohio, was the home of the only available military wind tunnel east of the Mississippi River. It was the equivalent of a huge fan pushing air straight up and out a twenty foot diameter tunnel. The top of the tunnel was covered with a net to keep anyone from actually falling into the running fan and making a mess. This fan generated wind speed to replicate the wind resistance generated during a free fall. This allowed you to dive into the wind tunnel and practice body positioning techniques to get stable. At the end of your turn you extended your arms and the wind pushed you back to the edge and out of the tunnel. Each student got two turns in the tunnel and had to demonstrate an ability to get stable in the air. Then it was back to Fort Bragg.

The return trip to Fort Bragg would be our first actual Military Free Fall Jump. We would jump from 13,000 feet and open at 3,500. Students were paired by body weight with an equal sized instructor. This instructor would jump with them to ensure they were not totally out of control. If you couldn't get stable and pull your ripcord on time you were considered a safety hazard and dropped from the course.

I sat with my parachute on my back and had serious apprehension about the jump that was just minutes away. All of the students were fidgeting and putting on a brave face. The ramp of the plane opened and my group of jumpers moved to the edge. I had a birds-eye view of the ground thirteen-thousand feet below and the world was spread out for all to see. All of the jokes about taking that "big step" off the back of the aircraft were put aside. It was a hell of a long way down.

The Jumpmaster made a fist and held up his extended thumb to signify, "Get Ready." Then he extended his arm and fingers to point out the back of the aircraft. This was the command to

"GO!" For a half second I paused, then just dove off the ramp. The 140 knot winds caught me and threw me like a rag doll out into the heavens. I thought to myself, *Arch, Arch, Arch,* as I spread my hands and feet. I arched my back to get stable in the rush of air. In a few seconds the forward momentum of the aircraft subsided and a downward plunge ensued. As the speed of descent increased so did a wall of wind resistance. This provided a wave of air to get my body stabilized. Now I could actually get a feel for what was happening.

*A C-141 ramp jump.*

The first jump was an indoctrination into a strange and new environment. Once you had taken "the step" you knew what to expect in the jumps to follow. The anxiety and nervousness were still there, but little by little they started to fade. Each jumper gradually gained confidence in his ability and equipment.

Up to 12,999 feet above sea level, oxygen was not required. From 13,000 to 17,999 feet, you needed supplemental oxygen. This was the equivalent of passing around an oxygen bottle and each jumper sucking in a few breaths. From 18,000 to 24,999 feet, each jumper had to be hooked to an oxygen console and pre-breathe to remove the nitrogen from his system.

We executed a few combat equipment jumps from 18,000 feet. Then it was time to jump from 25,000 feet. The pilots said that on a clear day you could see the Atlantic coastline from Fort Bragg. As I exited, I looked for the coast but could not get a glimpse of it. What I did see was the ground—a long way down there. It was the first time our altimeters, worn on our wrist, had to go around twice. I kept glancing at it to make sure I didn't lose track. I fell and fell and it gave me a lot of time to work on "flying."

In the end, I made twenty-eight jumps during the school and made a lot of friends. Each pair of jumpers was assigned an instructor for safety and to teach them the techniques to improve in the air. I learned a couple years later that my instructor had experienced a malfunction doing a hook turn (a quick turn under canopy) and crashed into the ground breaking both of his legs. I never heard if he recovered and returned to duty.

\*     \*     \*

Twice each year the Fire Support Platoon would fly to Viequez Island, Puerto Rico, for Naval Gunfire Training. Viequez Island is a very small chunk of land that sits off the eastern coast of Puerto Rico. It measures about two miles wide by four miles long and has a very sparse population.

This out of the way island had the most unspoiled and beautiful beaches I had ever seen. I had been to Megan's Beach on St. Thomas, which was rated one of the ten most beautiful beaches in the world, and it did not compare to Viequez Island. The water was deep green and blue and we took every opportunity to conduct swim "training."

A half-mile from the front gate is a little town called Esperanza. It sits right on a white sand beach with bright blue water lapping the shores. Across the narrow beach front street was a strip of little wooden cantina's with thatched or tin roofs. Each of them had a veranda from which to sit and have a drink and look out across the water. It was a beautiful and quaint setting that you would have to visit to appreciate. Words can not do it justice.

On the eastern end of the island was a naval gunnery range, which was the real reason we jumped onto the island each year. A naval ship would position itself off the southern coast of the island and we would adjust their fires onto targets. Often, we would combine mortar, naval gunfire, attack helicopter, and AC-130 Specter Gunship fires training.

It was the best of both worlds. Good and hard training combined with a beautiful tropical environment. At night we would look across the ocean to the east and see the lights of St. Croix. Most nights we could see the cruise ships with glistening lights as they passed between the islands. The whole place just made you feel very alive.

During the gunnery training we would try to hit large yellow vehicles that had been placed on the range as targets. Local ranchers let their cows wander on the range to find better pastures. These cows routinely hung out around the vehicles using the targets as scratching posts. Of course, an immediate goal became hitting one of those cows. We had a grand idea to remove a hindquarter from the carcass and have a beach barbeque. Hitting one of these cows became a very difficult and frustrating affair.

To appreciate the difficulty you must understand that a naval gun fires a five-inch round at a very high velocity. It is extremely accurate in deflection (left and right) but has a large range dispersion. It is the equivalent of shooting a rifle—the round travels flat and fast. Therefore, on flat ground, even small adjustments up or down resulted in a considerable change in range.

Those damned cows would be scratching away on the yellow targets and we would call in the gunfire. If we shot four rounds, two rounds would land short and the other two would land long, with a second in between. The smoke and dirt would fly and there would be the cows moseying off into the underbrush all fat and happy. I made eight trips to Puerto Rico and saw hundreds of rounds fly onto that gunnery range. We never did have that barbeque.

\*     \*     \*

In 1988, training missions began to take a specific focus toward raids on compounds, building clearing, and Military Operations in Urban Terrain (MOUT). Whenever a trend developed in training, it wasn't hard to check the newspapers to associate a place in the world to the training at hand. This time, riots and corruption in Panama fit the training scenarios.

At the time, I lived with Sergeant (SGT) Art Janes who worked in the Regimental Headquarters. I noticed he began to take his work and personal affairs a bit more seriously. Art Janes had always been a bit strange (he would laugh at that) but I had known him for years and considered him a reliable friend. I would ask him what was up at work, but he was a rock of secrecy. That meant something was afoot.

Unknown to us in the Ranger Battalions, a mockup of the Panamanian Commendancia had been built at Camp Blanding, Florida. The replica was complete with the outer wall and buildings. Days later, we began a series of practice missions to work out the plan for possible action in Panama. The mission called for us to fly right into Panama City and fast rope directly on to strategic buildings. We would emplace snipers and anti-tank guns to isolate the objective. No one would get in or out. Simultaneously, a larger assault force would land, breach the wall, and clear the objective.

On the first rehearsal mission, a major debate developed over how we were going to get through that rock wall after the compound was surrounded. It was finally decided that I would use an LPL-30 Laser Pointer to mark the desired location of the breach on the exterior of the wall. A backup method would be a ball of chemical lights thrown against the wall. Then I would call forward two attack helicopters, which would use 2.75mm rockets to blow a hole in the wall.

The use of the LPL-30 was a proven practice, but there was concern that too much light in the area, combined with trees, could make the spot hard to see for the pilots. Therefore, the idea of chemical lights was thrown in. That part was totally ridiculous as it would be a Kamikaze mission to run to the wall. During a rehearsal we tested the idea and I ran forward under covering fire and "threw" the chemical light bundle. I was so laden with body armor, weapon, and other gear that my effort did not even reach the wall. It turned out the distance to the wall was too far from any reasonable cover and concealment.

The main lesson learned from that rehearsal was the chemical lights were not a good idea and we had better rely on the LPL-30 and tracer fire if needed. Also, there was speculation that the 2.75mm rockets could not blow a big enough hole to do any good. The pilots were confident the rockets would do the job, but the Ranger planners remained unconvinced.

That rehearsal mission was again costly. Numerous Rangers were hurt fast-roping onto buildings. One Ranger missed the rope completely and fell eighty feet to the ground. His weapon, a Squad Automatic Weapon (SAW), ripped the side of his face off. He also broke both femurs and bit off his tongue. Apparently, he planned to fast-rope with his PVS-7 NVGs on and the resulting loss of depth perception caused him to lose his grip on the rope. His Ranger career was ended for good.

\*      \*      \*

The Battalion Combat Observation Lasing Teams (COLT) needed a Military Freefall (MFF) Jumpmaster to ensure we could always execute independent missions regardless of any outside support. It was decided that I would attend this course as one of the first carrots dangled in front of my face to convince me to re-enlist. I was six months out from my reenlistment window and the Company Commander was trying to keep his team together.

I made the familiar trip to Fort Bragg with a Ranger buddy who was attending the Army Sniper School at the same time. A few of my other friends were already at the Special Warfare Center (SWC). They were attending the basic MFF course and I expected our off-time to make this a fun trip.

*Military Freefall Training, Dugway, Utah.*

A MFF Jumpmaster was responsible for planning the jump, coordinating the release point with the aircraft pilot and navigator, inspecting the equipment and the aircraft, calculating the wind speed and drift of jumpers while "flying" in the air and under canopy, and putting the jumpers out of the aircraft. In static line jumps the chance of a miscalculation was small. In military freefall jumps many variables could easily be miscomputed or completely overlooked.

The release point is the spot on the ground where the jumpers exit the aircraft. Forward momentum carried you three hundred meters forward, until the speed generated from the aircraft diminished, and then the downward plunge began. During the fall, high altitude winds could blow the jumpers a considerable distance even before they opened their parachute. Once under canopy, lower altitude winds had a severe effect on the jumper's ability to steer to the drop zone. Winds at each of these levels had to be measured and calculated correctly.

Spotting release points from 13,000 feet, in the daylight, was one thing. To spot them from 18,000 feet at night was a different issue. Also, at 25,000 feet what looks like a small error in spotting the release point is actually a large distance on the ground. That distance can make all other calculations useless. The jumpers would never make it to the drop zone and be forced to land in any opening clear of trees and wires.

MFF Jumpmaster School was an advanced school and presented a real challenge. It had a reputation of requiring maximum attention to detail and produced a very bad attrition rate. I was an experienced jumper and had never had a problem in any school. Therefore I was confident I would be successful.

*Jumpmaster Students breathing oxygen in the aircraft.*

The class began and the days were spent inspecting jumpers, equipment, conducting actions in the aircraft, familiarizing ourselves with MFF procedures and doing computation after computation.     Each day we would conduct jump operations and practice the techniques of talking the aircraft over the release point and then exiting the aircraft. We would get to the ground, repack our parachutes, and jump again.

Everything went smoothly until the final test—Jumpmaster Parachute Inspection (JMPI). This was the sticking point of the whole course and caused the high attrition rate. We waited outside a classroom and one by one entered into a small building to be tested.    Inside were four jumpers wearing different configurations of equipment to be inspected. You had to inspect these jumpers, find a deficiency, announce it as "WRONG!" and continue on to the end.    There was a four-minute time limit. This was a zero defect test and one miss meant you failed.

It was my turn. I cracked my knuckles and faced the jumpers. An instructor commanded, "GO!" and I began inspecting the jumpers. I zoomed through these guys smoothly finding and announcing gigs as I progressed. I completed inspecting the last jumper and knew I had passed. I was pumped up, made a fist, and victoriously exclaimed, "Yeah!"

The cadre said, "Jumper number three, turn around. Sergeant, take a look at the back of this jumper." I re-examined the jumpers parachute and saw nothing wrong. "Look at the pack closing sequence." The flaps had to close in a specific sequence and they were definitely wrong.

All I said was, "FUCK!"

"You failed the inspection but lucky for you this is the first class with a retest. You get to try again tomorrow morning at 0700."

I could not believe it. I had been so pumped minutes before but now had the life sucked right out of me. I returned to the barracks totally depressed and stopped by Staff Sergeant Mallon's room. He was a friend from my Company attending the basic course and I told him what had happened. He actually thought it was funny because I had been so confident heading into it. I got no sympathy there, so I stopped by the shoppette for something to eat. Still in a state of shock I went to my room to eat a whole quart of Rocky Road ice cream.

The next morning found me standing in front of those jumpers again. One of three instructors commanded, "GO!" and I beat the hell out of those jumpers. I spun them this way and that inspecting for gigs. I got to the end and was again pumped up—this time with a measure of caution. The head instructor paused, then said, "Jumper number three, turn around. Sergeant, what is wrong with this jumper?"

*Exiting both doors from a C-141 on a HALO jump.*

My heart sunk as I looked at and re-inspected his rig. I thought to myself, *I must have fucked it up again!* In an instant state of depression I said, "I don't know—I can't find anything."

He directed, "Look at the pack closing sequence."

I yelled at myself inside my head, *No way. You have got to be kidding me!* I re-inspected the closing sequence and found nothing wrong. "It's O.K."

"That's right, you passed!" The cadre started laughing, shaking my hand and slapping me on the back. I was numb and it took me a second to let it sink in. I had passed the course and was damned glad it was over. I was a MFF Jumpmaster.

\*     \*     \*

In February of 1989, the Reenlistment NCO stopped me and asked if I wanted to "Re-up." God, all I had thought about for four years was getting out. I'd kept telling myself not to get too wrapped up in this Army "stuff" because there was a lot to do on the outside. I tried to deny it, but I actually was starting to love what I did here. The first few years of any enlistment were generally spent thinking about friends, girls, and family back home. Gradually the strength of those feelings faded and you realized "home" would never be the same. Your buddies were getting married, hanging out in the same old bar, or maybe moved away to pursue their own lives and careers. That big place you grew up in now seemed pretty small.

Professionally you paid your dues during those first four years and gained experience and rank. The rank garnered more responsibility and respect from everyone you worked with. I had worked hard in a very competitive and demanding environment, just like all my buddies, and I didn't want to throw that away.

I hemmed and hawed for a few weeks and finally, while sitting on the beach in Panama City, Florida, I made my decision. Doug Fenske and I had a four-day pass and were having a blast chasing girls by the ocean. I said to Doug over a beer on the beach, "What are we going to do if we get out? The same thing as we were doing before we came in?" I knew I wasn't going back home to a boring job or to sit behind a desk. That decided it for me—I would reenlist.

*Ranger Buddies in 1988 at 3/75 Ranger Battalion.*

We returned from the weekend and Lieutenant Joe Adams met me at the door of the office. Joe was my Company Fire Support Officer and immediate supervisor. "SGT Combs, do you want to reenlist?"

"I don't know Sir. What will I get?"

"The Commander says you can have your choice of Pathfinder or Scuba School and a four day pass."

"O.K, I'll take Pathfinder School and I want my four day pass during spring break. I've got a friend coming to visit."

He replied with a big smile, "You mean you'll do it?"

"You give me Pathfinder School and I'll reenlist, Sir." That was that.

After my four-day pass, SFC Keith asked if I wanted to move over to the 75th Ranger Regiment Fire Support Element to work on the COLT teams. I wasn't too happy with my situation in A-Company of 3rd Ranger Battalion. I had been the Company Fire Support Sergeant and felt I had done a good job.

I was an E-5 in an E-6 slot and replaced when a new E-6 arrived at the Battalion. The E-6 washed out within three months of arriving. By that time I had already requested to move to the 75th Ranger Regimental Headquarters. CPT Thomas then asked me to take the job again. It was expected I would reassume the job. I said, "I'm sorry, sir, but you replaced me. I'm going to Regiment to be the Senior Fire Support Sergeant."

\*     \*     \*

In April of 1989, I moved to the 75th Ranger Regimental Headquarters. As a Sergeant (E-5), I would be the Senior Fire Support Sergeant, until a Sergeant First Class (SFC) could be found to fill the slot. SFC Keith held the position and was moving on to Alaska. Sergeant (SGT) Art Janes was preparing to transition to civilian life. I needed to find some good people to get my team together.

When I arrived, there were two solid Private First Classes already at the Regiment. Then I persuaded SGT Leonard Jones and SSG Fenske into joining the team. That gave us five very strong, experienced, and motivated Rangers.

Our mission would be twofold. First, to assist the two Regimental Fire Support Officers (FSO) in providing all fires from mortar, artillery, attack helicopters, Naval Gunfire and Close Air Support for the Regiment. Our other mission was to train a Ranger COLT team at the Regimental level. This would give the commander a viable option for the execution of deep strike missions.

Immediately after moving to the Regimental Headquarters, the riots in Panama turned violent and the Regiment was alerted. It looked like the situation had deteriorated enough for the United States to intervene. The entire Regiment prepared to deploy and then waited for the movement order. The situation in Panama cooled off again and we returned to a normal training schedule.

*Ranger COLT (left to right) myself, Doug, and Art Janes.*

The Fire Support Element focus during this time was to train a competent and deployable COLT. The Ranger COLT concept had made many changes during the previous years and numerous team configurations proposed. The Regiment required an effective deep strike capability and we made this a training priority for the next six months. I basically had a free hand to execute the training I felt we needed. The first exercise was an airborne insertion onto McKenna airstrip on Fort Benning. We jumped, assembled, and conducted a tough twelve-mile infiltration to Kilo Impact area. There we lased targets for incoming A-10 Warthogs.

The standard operation was to infiltrate into the target area, occupy a hide site, recon a lase site with an unobstructed view of the target, and wait for the preplanned arrival of the planes. At that time, we would move into position, establish a one word code with the pilot, and mark the target with the AN/PAQ-1 Laser Target Designator.

*Military Free Fall Training, Norton AFB, CA (personal photo)*

This mission concept was practiced with a number of variations. We would infiltrate by zodiac boat, foot, vehicle, helicopter, static line parachute, and High Altitude/Low Opening (HALO) or High Altitude/Low Opening (HAHO) operations. HALO and HAHO were the military equivalent of sky diving, with full combat equipment and oxygen, to achieve altitudes up to thirty-thousand feet.

In HAHO you opened your parachute after a seven second delay at altitudes up to eighteen-thousand feet. This allowed you to use the parachute as a glider and ride the high altitude winds far behind enemy lines. Extraction was almost always via a helicopter pickup zone or the Small Patrol Infiltration or Exfiltration Rig (SPIE).

Use of the SPIE Rig consisted of using a radio to verbally direct a helicopter over a hole in the trees. It was always assumed there would be obstructions such as trees, rocks, or power lines that would prevent the helicopter from landing on the ground. The Load Master would then drop a large wool rope with interwoven D-rings through the forest canopy to the patrol on the ground. Each member of the patrol put on a harness with a single strap that ran from behind the neck to a snap-ring. When the pilot dropped the rope, team members hooked into the rope in pairs. Then the helicopter began to rise straight up. The bottom man used a radio to talk to the pilot and reported when the bottom man had cleared the trees. When the pilot heard, "CLEAR!" He eased the helicopter forward and gradually accelerated. The wind drag created a powerful G-Force on the bottom man and made for a painful ride!

\*    \*    \*

The same year we deployed to Fort Campbell, Kentucky to conduct HALO training with the 5th Special Forces Group. We would make a series of jumps day and night up to 18,000 feet to get Level One proficiency training. This meant a unit fully trained, refreshed and ready to conduct any operation. The jumps would be from CH-47 Chinook helicopters and everyone looked forward to the training.

*COLT exiting a CH-47.*

To this point I had considered myself to be a pretty good "Air Commando" but a new respect for the danger involved was coming my way. Our training usually started slowly with easy jumps and gained speed and difficulty as the week progressed. The difficulty came from the addition of weapons, rucksacks, oxygen masks and bottles, and of course high altitudes and night operations.

With all of the dangerous training a Ranger conducts over a period of years, he gradually becomes desensitized to the associated fear and nervousness. Facing that fear time after time until it becomes routine is the purpose of training. It is only the unforeseen and untrainable equipment failure that disrupted that groove.

It had become routine to sit in a CH-47 helicopter with all my gear attached, an oxygen mask on my face, and to pre-breathe pure oxygen to remove nitrogen from the blood stream. The body vented this nitrogen through belching into the mask and farting which left the general area with a foul stench. The aircraft would take off and begin a flight route while gaining altitude to the target drop zone. Enroute, each jumper would make the final adjustment of his equipment and await the jump commands. The Jumpmaster would move about in the aircraft under the illumination of red lights and assume his position on the ramp. He then squatted to peer over the edge in the direction of flight. He must identify landmarks and ultimately the release point. About five minutes out, he motions for the jumpers to stand up, turn on your bail out bottle, disconnect from the console, and move to the rear of the aircraft.

At one minute, the Jumpmaster bumps a fist on the floor then raises a thumb up for all to see. The jumpers move to the edge of the ramp. The Jumpmaster then stands, puts an arm across his chest and then points off the ramp. That meant, "GO!" The team would dive in unison off the ramp and into the blackness of the night.

A split second off the ramp, the 100-knot winds, produced by the forward speed of the aircraft, tossed each jumper like a leaf. Soon that forward speed subsided and a downward plunge began. The difficulty in this situation is the darkness, which makes it difficult to keep track of your teammates in the air. Each jumper had a chemical light stick on his leg but at that speed it was hard to keep each other in sight. With practice and experience this could be considered a routine event but one night I had a problem.

I had been having trouble getting one of my rucksack attaching straps to seat and lock into position. During my final adjustment I got it to lock and moved to the ramp with the other jumpers. All was O.K. until I left the ramp at which time my right attaching strap came completely loose. The corresponding shoulder strap, wrapped around my right leg, also came apart. This left my rucksack free to buffet in the wind and threw me out of control. I couldn't "fly" and in the darkness strained to see what had happened. I was tumbling and buffeting as I attempted to adjust my body position to counter the flapping rucksack. I had to get stable or I would not be able to pull my ripcord. The pilot chute could come out and wrap around my body or the rucksack. To make matters worse I had gotten a boot to the face upon exit which unseated my mask up into my broken goggles. Falling completely out of control, in the pitch black of night, with a weapon, rucksack, and oxygen mask restricting your vision was no small matter.

I gave up trying to "fly" and just reached between my legs and grabbed for my remaining attaching strap. After a short period I got a hand on the loose side of my rucksack, pulled it in and scissored it tightly between my legs. Next, I arched hard to get flat and then immediately pulled my ripcord. The chute opened and I was very irritated. When I looked in the mirror that night the evidence was there. I had the blood-red eyes of a vampire. This was the result of broken corpuscles from the G-forces of spinning out of control.

\*     \*     \*

One evening I decided to go with three buddies to Muldoon's, which was an Irish Pub on the north side of Columbus, Georgia. We partied there until about 1 a.m. when I suggested that we go get some breakfast and make sure we stayed out of trouble. We left the pub and drove to Shoney's breakfast bar off exit four near the Crossroads Mall. We sat with two guys on each side of the table and proceeded to dig in. Behind us, on my side of the table, was a man facing our direction. On our side of his table were his wife and young son.

I heard him say something about kicking GI's asses and sending them back to Fort Benning. I leaned across the table and whispered to my buddies that we might have to fight our way out of there because of what I was hearing behind me. Van Schmoll, a man not known for his late night tact, said, "Who, that Hitler-looking fuck?"

The guy was on his feet in a second and threatening to teach our whole table a lesson. I stood up, faced the guy and told him to calm down. I didn't even see his hands move and before I knew it I was sitting in my chair. He had hit me twice with a heavy ceramic coffee mug - once on the left cheekbone and once on the left side of my forehead. I don't remember much from those first few seconds but the other guys said he jumped back into a Karate position. I sprang off my chair and ran him over with a chest high tackle. Patrons screamed as his head bounced off the food bar and jell-o and eggs flew everywhere.

He went limp for a second as I was so angry I punched him a few times in the face. As I continued my attack, blood appeared on his face, but I couldn't see where it was coming from. Then I realized it was falling off of me. He had opened a big gash on my forehead and it was bleeding in a stream of droplets over everything.

My whole face and shirt were covered in blood and since I thought I had subdued this guy I sat back on my haunches and things started to get a little hazy. About this time the dude on the floor screamed with rage. I was losing speed—he was gaining it. Van Schmoll walked over and kicked the guy in the face with his right foot, which had a cast on it, and calmed him down again.

Two guys stood me up and dragged me toward the exit door. As we left the building the third buddy pulled up my truck. They threw me in, dove in after me, and we headed for Martin Army Hospital. Another Ranger in the breakfast bar witnessed the entire incident. Later, he said the police arrived just after we departed and arrested the guy and his family. In the meantime, we were racing toward the hospital because I wasn't looking too good.

We burst through the doors of the emergency room and a kid sitting with his mother exclaimed, "OH, COOL!" I looked down at myself and the front of my shirt was red with blood. The emergency staff threw me on a gurney and the doctor inspected the gash. He said my skull was dented but I would be all right. After three layers of five stitches, they sent me home with some good painkillers. I had a severe concussion and the left side of my face swelled up like a watermelon. I was put on a physical profile for two weeks to ensure I wouldn't do any activity that would aggravate my head wound.

Just after the profile ended, my COLT team was scheduled to execute a SPIE rig extraction out of KILO impact area and all the way to Lawson Army Airfield. As usual, I was the bottom man and used a radio to talk to the pilot. The ride was twenty-five miles and much longer than necessary. The guys wanted to fly over post on the rope to show off a bit.

About ten minutes into the flight I started to get sick. My head started to spin and I thought I was going to vomit all over myself. I closed my eyes tried to relax, but it didn't help. I called the Load Master and said, *"We have to set it down."*

He replied, *"Set it down?"*

*"This is COLT Team Leader, set it down, NOW!"*

We landed at Leah Field on the Alabama side of Benning, and I was so sick I thought I would die. I had a bad case of vertigo and vomit was sitting in the back of my throat. We loaded into the bird and flew the rest of the way back to post. Later that day I was diagnosed as having a severe concussion and for the next few months would experience bouts of vertigo and headaches before it finally faded away. I was left with a big scar on my forehead from trying to do the right thing.

# Chapter 4
## Operation Blue Spoon
### (Just Cause)

In November of 1989, I flew to Fort Bragg with Colonel (COL) "Buck" Kernan, the Regimental Commander, and Major (MAJ) Bob Click, the Regimental Assistant Fire Support Officer. MAJ Click was actually a Marine Liaison officer who functioned as the Assistant FSO. I hadn't officially been told a thing about what was to happen at Fort Bragg except to take a radio and be prepared to stay a couple days. On the flight up, I had a conversation with COL Kernan about my plans to go to Officer's Candidate School (OCS). COL Kernan was an OCS graduate and encouraged me to pursue the opportunity. I told him it was a tough decision because I had the best job in the Army. He just smiled.

When we arrived at Fort Bragg, we moved immediately to the 18th Airborne (ABN) Corps Headquarters. We were cleared through the security doors and moved to a small planning room. The conversation immediately turned to linkup procedures between the 82nd ABN and the Ranger Regiment and Command and Control responsibilities.

MAJ Click turned to me and said, "Do you have any questions?"

I said, "Sir, it's hard to have any questions when you haven't seen the plan."

That night we moved to a restricted compound where the 82nd Readiness Brigade was assembled. I watched the 82nd brief its plan to the Division Commander. It was my first look at a Division Commander. He walked in, let his gear fall on the floor, and slumped into his chair. The whole time everyone else in the room stood at attention. The room was completely silent.

We listened to the plan and then moved to prepare for the jump the next night.

Our Ranger cell dropped in first to simulate the Rangers on the ground in Panama. We were to secure the airhead for the arrival of the 82nd which would come in at H + one hour. H-hour is the time the operation begins. Soon the 82nd began to arrive. Forty-eight heavy drops preceded the jumpers and the night sky was soon filled with parachutes.

Everywhere I went I always carried my Gerber BMF (Big Mother Fucker) knife across my hip like a small sword. This night was no different. An 82nd Colonel walked up and said, "What are you going to do with that pig-sticker, Sergeant?"

I looked him straight in the eye and said, "Cut stuff, sir."

He smiled and said, "I'll see you in Panama." Then he moved off into the night.

The entire plan to link up on the ground and hand over Command and Control to the 18th ABN Corps went off without a hitch. We returned to Fort Benning the next day and began to prepare for the dress rehearsal to be executed in early December. The fact that it was a rehearsal for Panama was "close hold" and "need to know" information. Therefore, I could not disclose any details to my team when I returned to Fort Benning. It didn't take a rocket scientist to see that U.S. military action was imminent. There was increased news footage of political upheaval and riots in the streets of Panama. Also, several stories were aired concerning the security of the canal and safety of American citizens. All indications were President Bush would be forced to commit forces soon.

By December 1989, the team had shrunk to four Rangers—myself, SSG Fenske, SGT Jones, and SP4 Paul Hussein. Doug and I were still together and he had reenlisted to come from the 3rd Ranger Battalion to the Regiment. SGT Leonard Jones was my first RTO three years earlier. SP4 Paul Hussein had been at the Regimental Headquarters when I arrived. He was going through a hazing period because of the irony of his given name. This was not a good time to have the name Hussein. Saddam Hussein was getting plenty of press time and Paul was not amused. Regardless, he had proven that he could execute whatever mission was thrown his way.

It is hard to relate what a high quality team we had at that time. Not only were the members tough with an average PT score of 296 out of 300 but they were smart as well. The four team members had three Bachelors Degrees and one Associates Degree to their credit. We also had developed a cohesion that only resulted from executing many months of intense training.

Since I couldn't release any information on Panama, I started a crash refresher on airfield seizures, weapon systems of the Third World, country vehicle recognition, and communication equipment. The team wasn't foolish; they knew the deal. The rehearsal mission was executed in early December and drew a lot of attention because Airborne School Instructors were used as the Jumpmasters on the birds. That was totally out of the ordinary. So was the complete manifesting of the Ranger Indoctrination Program cadre for the Regimental Headquarters security element. The rehearsal went well and validated the plan that had been in development for years.

After the rehearsal mission, I gathered the team into the office and said, "Listen. I know it's time for Christmas leave but I recommend you think about staying here for the holidays. It's just a hunch, but you might want to think about it."

It turns out I had picked the day of the alert exactly. It was a Sunday morning and I decided to go deer hunting one last time for the year. I had my beeper with me so I had no fear of missing a call in the woods. Within a half-hour of leaving the truck, I had shot a big doe, field dressed it, and rushed it to the house to process before evening.

I was tired as hell. I told myself that I needed to finish the deer and catch a nap. My girlfriend asked why I didn't just leave it until the next day. I said I didn't think I'd be around to finish it. I threw the last piece of venison in the freezer and dove into bed. I had been lying down for about fifteen minutes when the phone rang. "Sergeant, this is a Bravo Notification. We are assembling." I looked at my girlfriend and my roommate Matt Brown and said, "I need to go to work." They knew immediately what was up and we said we would see each other later.

I walked to the Regimental fence and SGT Jones met me at the gate. "The Major says this one's for real. We're going to kick some ass!"

I said, "What's our status?"

"Hussein is drawing equipment and maps and we can't get hold of SSG Fenske," Jones said.

"Okay, keep trying to get SSG Fenske. I'm going to see the Major."

I went to see MAJ Newnam and he confirmed what Jones had told me. This one was for real. I headed directly back to the office and was met with bad news. SSG Fenske had left on leave to Iowa. It was an eighteen hour trip, and there was no way to get in touch with him in time. He wouldn't know a thing was happening until he saw it on the morning news in Iowa.

The Regiment always stands ready to deploy at a moment's notice, so it was business as usual to draw our equipment, maps, and conduct communications checks. The only difference was the issue of the Panama maps which we quickly acetated (applied clear durable lamination). We had one for each member of the team. My map covered Torrios Tecumen International Airport. I would jump there with MAJ Click and Team Gold. Since we were one man short, I would not have an

RTO. MAJ Newnam, SGT Jones, and SP4 Hussein would jump into Rio Hato with Team Black. Rio Hato was the location of Manuel Noriega's beach house and the Panamanian Defense Forces main barracks.

Around midnight, Team Gold began loading onto buses for the trip to Hunter Army Airfield. We would join the 1st Ranger Battalion and one Company from the 3rd Ranger Battalion. The Regimental Fire Support Team met in the office one last time. We gave each other the thumbs up and joked about seeing each other on the drop zone. It was a good team.

We arrived at Hunter Army Airfield in the early hours of the morning and moved directly into Saber Hall. It was that same familiar star shaped building as the operation moved underground. Everywhere I looked there were familiar faces. The Ranger Regiment was a very small and tight knit unit. It seemed the handshakes were coming from every direction.

It sends a chill down my spine to think of it. The feeling in the air was electric. The mission, for which we had trained for two years, was finally here. I remember SFC Tony Lewis shaking my hand and saying, "Man, this is some shit, isn't it?!"

No rehearsals and no distractions—it was all business. I obtained my copy of the aerial imagery and ran over the mission in my head time after time. COL Koran, the Deputy Commander of the Regiment, came into the room and walked the group through the operation one last time.

We took a break long enough to draw ammunition and immediately moved to make final communication checks and final preparations of personal equipment. Then we rigged the rucksacks for the upcoming airborne jump. I had drawn 210 rounds of 5.56mm ball ammunition, four fragmentation grenades and eight M-203 grenades for target marking. My personal weapon was a CAR-15 assault rifle with an M-203 grenade launcher specially rigged to attach underneath.

We headed back to the small briefing room where COL Koran briefed us one last time, "Rangers, the next time we see each other it will be on the drop zone in Panama. Let's all remember why we're here. Recognizing that I volunteered as a Ranger ..." and he led us in the Ranger Creed. I remember the hairs on the back of my neck standing up as the reality of the moment sunk in.

We marched in a downpour to the waiting C-141 Starlifter transport planes just after dark. When we reached our bird, we quickly loaded the parachutes waiting on the ramp to keep them dry. We then loaded ourselves and personal equipment. I had just been seated by the Safety when it was determined our bird was broken. We would have to move to the "Bump" bird (spare). We quickly transferred all our gear to the other bird about one-hundred yards away and sat down for the seven hour flight.

At that time, planes began taking off from both Hunter Army Airfield, in Savannah, and Lawson Army Airfield, at Fort Benning. My roommate, Captain Matt Brown, later told me that he stood on the balcony of the apartment and listened to the planes taking off. They turned and flew directly over Phoenix City, Alabama on their way to the southwest. He said it was an eerie feeling knowing what was soon to take place.

The flight route took us across Texas to the Pacific to avoid detection by Cuban radars and down the western side of Mexico. Once we reached Panama, we would make a large looping turn to the east and then approach the drop zone from the south.

It was a seven-hour flight that each individual endured in his own way. Some Rangers dosed, some poured over maps and photos and some prayed. I personally reflected on my life, my family, and made my peace with God. The remainder of the time I said a special little prayer, "God, I hope they don't call it off!"

Roughly three hours out, we began to in-flight rig the Rangers for the jump.  I inspected more than my share of jumpers to ensure I would have the latest possible opportunity to relieve myself at the urinal one last time.

At one hour out, the Jumpmaster came on the intercom saying, *"Rangers it will be a "HOT" drop zone.  It was reported on the News that planes are taking off at Fort Bragg. They will be waiting for us!"*

"Twenty minutes!" screamed the Jumpmasters.

"Twenty Minutes!" the jumpers answered back in unison. At twenty minutes, all jumpers were awake and alert.  The jump lights by the door came on.  Both red and green appeared as the Loadmaster made sure they were functional.  Then the green turned off and the red remained.

"Ten Minutes!" screamed the Jumpmasters.

"Out board personnel, stand up!"

"In board personnel, stand up!"

"Hook Up!"

"Check Static Lines!"

"Check Equipment!"

"Sound off for equipment check!"

"All O.K., Jumpmaster!"

Then the Jumpmaster took control of the door.

This was a combat jump and the Jumpmaster would lead out the door.  There would be one pass and one pass only.  If you didn't get out, you were going to read about it in the paper.  The wind speed was 140 knots at 500 feet.  I was lucky.  I was the fourth man, right door, on the seventh bird.  I was definitely going to get out.

The last few minutes of any Combat Equipment jump were extremely painful.  The equipment cut into your shoulders and crotch and gave you an incredible backache. The pain becomes so consuming that you could not wait to get out of the bird. At three minutes the doors came open. The familiar howl of the wind deflectors extending to push the rush of air away from the jump doors could be heard by everyone on board. I could immediately feel the warm, damp tropical air and I positioned myself inward so I could see out the jump doors. I could see the lights of Panama City as we came "feet dry" off the ocean.

"One Minute! Let's go and get some, Rangers!" screamed the Jumpmaster.

"Thirty Seconds!" The plane jerked violently as the pilot made a last second adjustment or jockeyed to avoid enemy fire. The quick shift threw the jumpers off balance.

Green Light, the Jumpmaster screamed, "GO!" then lead the way out the door. The plane shifted again and you could hear the engines ROAR as the pilot accelerated. I was thrust so fast toward the rear of the aircraft that I hit the door jam and just threw myself sideways out of the door. I didn't even bother to count to see if my main parachute opened on time. If my parachute totally malfunctioned I didn't think I'd have time to deploy my reserve anyway.

The parachute deployed with a violent jerk due to the speed of the aircraft. I found myself spinning all the way up my risers. I said to myself, "Ah fuck! Ah fuck!" as I pulled wide on my risers and tried to stop the spinning. I finally stopped the twisting up and started twisting the other way. I could hear small arms fire in the distance but nothing too close at that time. I tried to get my bearings in the air by getting a good look at the airfield on the way down but it was impossible with the spin I was in.

During each rotation of the spin, I also desperately tried to see the ground in the direction my parachute was drifting. With the twists in the risers, I had absolutely no control of the parachute and no choice where I landed. To make matters worse, there was every possibility a Panamanian could be waiting to execute me as soon as I hit the ground. That was my worst nightmare along with the fact that I was out of control, no weapon in hand and not being able to see where I would land. The spinning continued, and that's how I hit the ground—spinning.

I crashed into the abutment of a bridge located outside the airhead fence on the Pan-American Highway. I hit the rock incline and somersaulted downward into the stream bed below. Because of my twists, I couldn't steer my parachute, and to make matters worse, I didn't see that bridge coming. I landed hard and for a second or two was totally disoriented as I lay in my harness. As soon as I regained my senses, I immediately pulled my rifle from the weapons case, slammed a magazine in the well and chambered a round. At that moment, three vehicles raced across the bridge above me heading away from the airfield. For days, I wouldn't realize the significance of those vehicles.

Next out was the BMF. I cut my parachute off and the rucksack free of its rigging straps. At the time, having to pay for damaged rigging just didn't seem too important. I then put my radio into operation and tried to establish communications with the Specter gunship overhead. I could hear him but I couldn't get a response to my commo check. I rechecked the handmike, antenna and frequencies but still couldn't talk. Due to the impact on the rocks I thought it possible my radio had lost its secure cipher fill. I decided to give it up and head for the assembly area.

I climbed out of the stream bed and saw what I thought was the exterior fence of the airfield. I found a hole, moved through it and ran into three Rangers hung up in the approach lights. They had just finished getting their gear on. We intended to move as a group into the airhead. As we began to move, they headed the opposite direction I was going to go. It turns out I was so disoriented, from twisting into my controlled crash into the bridge, that I would have moved in the wrong direction. In my haste to get moving, I had violated the cardinal rule learned in the desert years before—*always* pull out your compass and get your bearings before you move.

We moved about fifty yards through the kunta grass to the stream bed I had just come from and found the stream was too big to cross. Everyone on the other side of the stream was already gone. Because of the great amount of time we had wasted, I was concerned about running into the Ranger blocking positions moving in our direction. We could hear the 82nd Airborne's planes overhead and we needed to get moving. I dropped my rucksack and tried again to get Specter on the radio. If I could contact him, he could tell me what was on the other side of the gate. Again, I could hear but I couldn't talk.

At that moment I felt a tap on my shoulder. When I looked up, I saw a young Ranger pointing at a car that had stopped at the gate around seventy-five yards away. Alongside the car were two guards talking to the driver, one on our side of the car and one on the other side. I didn't know if the guards had come from the guardhouse at the gate or had gotten out of the car.

Decision time—were these guy's hostile or were they just night watchmen talking to their girlfriends. They did not appear to have weapons? If they did, it was at best a pistol. We were on the outside of the airhead late in the operation and shooting inward. I knew Rangers were preparing to come out that gate very soon. It's amazing how fast your mind works in this type of situation.

The female driver pulled away and the two guards stepped into the guardhouse. The entire time this had been transpiring I had kept the handmike in my ear and made a call for fire to Specter to engage Target Number 4. I got no reply but I then heard Specter say he was going to engage target number four. That was the guardhouse immediately to our front. I whispered to the other, "Get down. Specter is going to shoot this target right now."

Whether he heard me or saw the target for himself became immaterial. A few seconds later, a loud, short, and metallic explosion echoed loudly through the night and the guards were dead. I'm not sure if it was a 105mm or a 40 mm round but the effect was the same. Seconds after the explosion two Ranger Special Operations Vehicles burst through the gate and headed our direction. The vehicles moved down the road and one stopped on the other side of the bridge and the other moved across the bridge to our left. This was not a good position to be in again. We were in the wrong place and needed to link up. As the crew began to put out road blocks and barbed wire I moved over near the road. Then, when I was sure the M-60 gunners were looking the other direction, I yelled the running password, "BULLDOG!"

The jeep team echoed back, "BULLDOG!" and we climbed up onto the road. I quickly strode down the road to the other RSOV and stopped because a vehicle was approaching from the west toward our position. A Ranger from the RSOV said, "Here!" and handed me a Light Anti-Tank Weapon (LAW). Things were getting tense. I took off the covers, extended the LAW, shouldered it and waited for the vehicle. The vehicle approached the barricade that the teams just put out and then stopped. It hesitated for a second then turned around and headed off the other direction. I handed the LAW back to the RSOV, shouldered my rucksack and moved through the gate.

As I went by the guard shack, I glanced at the dead guards on the right and continued on my way to the east. They didn't seem too important right now. Just past the guardhouse was my first obstacle. I had to cross the runway and taxiway to continue moving east. The other Rangers had headed to the north to another objective. I began to feel particularly vulnerable as I tried to pull 360 degree security for myself.

I thought, *The hell with it, here I go.* Running as fast as I could across the concrete, I heard an explosion to my right and machine gun fire. Rounds snapped and whirred as I continued across. I didn't know if someone was shooting at me or they were just errant rounds coming from the airport terminal. Either way it had the same effect—I was moving out.

Another three-hundred meters down the road, I saw a patrol of about six to eight soldiers moving toward me in a tactical road march formation. Half of the patrol was on each side of the road. I continued to watch them through my Night Vision

Goggles and I could make out the bushy helmets of American soldiers. At about thirty meters they all moved off to the right side of the road and went into a gaggle. When no weapons appeared to be pointed in my direction, I yelled, "BULLDOG!"

The whole group jumped to their feet training their weapons in my direction. "Jesus Christ! This is the 75th Ranger Regiment Senior Fire Support Sergeant!" I yelled.

"Aw, come on up, bud." some one replied as they lowered their weapons.

"God damn! Didn't you hear me yell BULLDOG?" I said as I approached. I had come close to being killed by our own men.

"What's BULLDOG?" someone replied.

I was dismayed, "It's the running password!"

"It's not ours." they answered.

I though to myself, *Oh great! I'm moving around the airfield by myself and we don't even have the same running password.*

I then asked them, "Where are you guys headed?"

"Down this road to a gate." one soldier said.

"I just came from there and there's a Ranger blocking position just outside the gate."

"Hey, can you show us where we are on the map?"

"Yeah," I said as I pulled out my map, spread it on the ground and shined my red lens Maglite on it.

I pointed to our position on the map. "You guys are right here. You're going right there. Did you guys see any Rangers where you came from?" I asked.

One paratrooper pointed east, "Yeah, there's an Aid Station back down this road a ways. Hey, do you have an extra map?"

As I was putting on my gear I thought to myself, *You have got to be kidding. You're in a combat situation in a foreign country. You don't know the running password. You don't know where you're at and you don't have a map.* "Yeah, here have this one. I've got my aerial photo to work off of." We parted Company and headed in different directions. They moved to the west and I moved to the east.

I figured I had about four-hundred meters to go until I got to the location where our Tactical Operations Center (TOC) should have moved to. It is not a good feeling to be running around the airhead by yourself. I would move fifty meters, stop to look in all directions with my night vision goggles and then move again. Until I linked up, I felt that everyone was the enemy. Wouldn't it just suck to be shot by a friendly was all I thought as I tried to see any potential 'enemy' first. I continued down the road to a pump station and then moved off to the right toward the terminal. About two-hundred meters across a gully riddled grass field, I finally walked into the security for the Team Gold Regimental TOC. I found my way to Major Click. He was happy to see me.

"You all right?" he said.

"Yes sir, sorry I'm so late ... my radio's broke."

I then heard someone say, "God damn, we thought you got shot!" There was the smiling face of SFC Russell Peele. He was a hell of a good friend.

I replied, "No man, I just landed all fucked up," as we shook hands.

We stayed in that position until after daylight watching wave after wave of the 82nd Airborne get their 'combat jumps.' I heard some Rangers say, "Damn, why don't they just land?" In reality, it was quicker to unload the planes by jumping and allow the planes to continue on their way to refuel. Credit for a combat jump was a paratrooper 'thing.' "Do these guys get Combat Jump Stars?" we kept joking back and forth.

The major action of the night had taken place inside the airport terminal. Security guards had taken some tourists hostage and one had fled into a restroom. It had just been reported that we had a hostage situation when a young Ranger threw down his weapon, burst into the room and tackled the Panamanian Security Guard. No hostage situation.

The guy in the restroom was another matter. A Ranger fire team attempted to move into the restroom after him and the lead NCO was hit. His men pulled him out and threw a grenade back in. After the resulting explosion, the team burst into the room. The guard, apparently injured by the explosion, charged and grabbed a Ranger. Two Rangers joined the wrestling match, noting that the enemy guard was super strong and enraged. The situation ended with the guy being thrown out the latrine window and his head cracking open on the concrete below.

The 82nd Airborne troops assembled in chalk order on the infield of the runways. A few hours after day light, six CH-47 helicopters landed, picked them up and transported them to a target to conduct a raid. Everything to this point had transpired just as had been briefed and rehearsed at the coordination meeting at the 18th Airborne Corps headquarters before Thanksgiving.

After noon on the first day, everything was calm around the airhead so I went with another Ranger over to the airport terminal to take a look around. I moved through the terminal and noticed the shops had been looted of everything from books to liquor. We moved down into the basement and bumped into a casualty collection point I didn't know was there. Doctors were working on casualties and soldiers were laying on litters with IVs sticking into them. I remember focusing on one soldier just laying with an IV in his arm and staring at the ceiling. He looked so pissed off! I was thinking of talking to him, but as things were hectic, we just moved off and continued around the terminal area.

Later that day we moved from our position into an open building and remained there for two days. Most of that time was spent watching the 82nd try to retrieve their equipment from the swamps at the lead edge of the drop zone. Apparently something had gone wrong and the forty-eight heavy drops never made the drop zone. They landed in the swamps and wouldn't be located for days.

On the second day, the 7th Infantry Division from Fort Ord, California, arrived and took responsibility for the security of the airfield. The Rangers then moved to the airfield interior and readied themselves to be moved to Howard Air Force Base for follow-on missions. A humorous situation arose with the 7th ID. Late at night we would hear the explosion of a claymore mine being triggered followed by a huge rush of gunfire. Apparently, the positions would hear the sounds of the night jungle, trigger the mines and waste a lot of ammunition to find out there was no one there. On the other hand, better safe than sorry.

I think of that situation often and wonder if I should have shot the two guys and the female driver. I made the call for fire and the guards died anyway—so did the female later. In a combat situation, weapons discipline and careful selection of only hostile targets was foremost in your mind. The other option would have been to shoot one guy in the back as he talked to the driver. Then take a chance that the guy on the other side of the vehicle couldn't hit us in the kunta grass. That was all combined with an awareness that those jeep teams were coming out that gate any minute.

MAJ Click had a similar decision to make. He said he landed alongside the runway, was lying on his back, and had just put his weapon into operation, when a guy came walking right up to him. The Major pointed his weapon at him and he moseyed off the other direction. Apparently, it was some Panamanian guy just walking around and watching the show.

After the 7th Infantry Division had established blocking positions around the airhead, I grabbed SFC Peele and we went back to the location where I had landed by the bridge. As we walked out the gate, there was that old rusty Oldsmobile turned over on its top. Apparently, the female had tried to run the roadblock and get back to the guard post—she didn't make it.

We continued across the bridge. SFC Peele couldn't believe I had landed so far out. I climbed down into the streambed to retrieve my M-1950 weapons case and my 18-inch attaching straps. We moved back to the Command Post. The 7th ID had taken my parachute canopy and used it as a sun shade at a blocking position near the bridge.

That evening we loaded a CH-47 Chinook helicopter and flew to Howard Air Force Base to join the Regimental Command Post. There I linked up with Jones and Hussein who had jumped at the other target. We exchanged stories about what we had seen. Their drop zone had been hotter than ours and actively opposed by the Panamanian Defense Forces.

That was the location of the famous Stealth fighter bomber strike onto the barracks that landed between the two buildings and did not hit either. In the planning phases, the target was located on the building but now it was said the target was changed to land between the buildings. I seriously doubted it.

During the jump on Rio Hato, a Panamanian .50 cal MG was raking the drop zone trying to repel the invasion. SSG "Goose" Newberry and LT Loren Ramos both landed near the position in a slight depression. They got out of their gear, low crawled together up the slope, then rose up and silenced the gunner by shooting him in the head.

Armored vehicles, much like bank cars, attempting to roll onto the airfield were silenced by Light Anti-tank Weapons

(LAW) and small arms fire as the building clearing teams moved into the barracks and command post areas. The Rangers had been training for months to clear these buildings in the dark with the use of Night Vision Goggles (NVGs). As they approached, they found the lights remained on. A difficult lesson would be learned at the cost of a young Rangers life from the 2nd Ranger Battalion on this target. As a fire team stacked on the side of a building and prepared to clear it, the Ranger was shot from a position away from the building and along a tree line. The focus on the clearing of a building where the enemy was expected left an opportunity to be engaged from another direction. You can never cover all of the angles if the enemy is intent on taking his chances.

The days to follow were spent listening to reports of Rangers securing huge quantities of arms and ammunition and hunting for Noriega and his staff. We had a picture of each of his cronies posted on a bulletin board. As each one was caught we X'd him out with a big red pen.

We finally caught Noriega's bodyguard and he recounted what had happened on the night of the invasion. It turned out Noriega had been in the Torrios Tecumen Airport having sex with a whore when the jump began. When they heard the roar of the planes overhead, he ran with his guards to his vehicles and fled to the west to get away. Those were the vehicles that had zoomed over the bridge above me when I was getting out of my gear!

We remained at Howard for days. Each day was filled with planning for future targets and the possibility of future missions. Numerous times my team prepared to fly out to provide security for Regimental Command and Control teams and every time it was called off. It was a frustrating situation as everyone wanted to go where the action might be.

One evening I heard that the Regimental Reconnaissance Detachment (RRD) was planning to HALO into a remote area to provide landing zone security for raid teams inserted to secure the arms and ammunition the local militias were using. I went to see SFC Lane and sold the idea that they should include me in the jump. I had the experience to provide the fire support they may need to protect the LZ. The RRD agreed to the plan and made coordination to procure me a parachute. While we waited the entire plan was also called off.

In reality, no real action was taking place in country by this time. All organized resistance had either taken to the hills or had given up. For all intent and purpose the short lived *Just Cause* was over.

\* \* \*

I returned from Panama around 3 January 1990. The rear detachment Officer in Charge (OIC) met us at the plane with vehicles, loaded our gear, and told us to go home for the weekend. I talked with him for a short time about what had been going on at the Regiment while we were gone. He said that the RIP (Ranger Indoctrination Program) students were going to be the Regimental Reserve and committed if we took too many casualties. These Ranger candidates had just arrived from Airborne School or other units, were issued weapons and equipment, and taken to a hangar on Lawson Army Airfield. Once in the hangar, the new Rangers began to prepare their equipment. At the same time the cadre organized them into squads and platoons. The Ranger Cadre said the RIP candidates were so scared they could barely get their equipment together. They continued preparations and waited for the Situation Report (SITREP) to come via satellite communications from the drop zones in Panama. When the word came that the mission was a success and the reserve would not be needed, some of the students were so relieved they broke down and cried.

To someone who has not endured a similar situation the reaction of the soldiers might seem silly. Remember, these were soldiers who had been in the Army for approximately four months. They had immediately been thrust into an unfamiliar, stressful and intense environment. They had nothing to rely upon but the commands of their superiors.

The Ranger Regiment is ready to deploy 24 hours a day and 365 days a year. When they say they are ready, they are not kidding. Every Ranger is a deployable infantryman when called.

\*        \*        \*

On the next Monday, I arrived before sun up prepared to sign into Pathfinder School. I had tried for the past year to get a slot, and when I arrived, there was a huge crowd of soldiers hoping to get into the class. Since it was a lucrative school, many soldiers would come on 'standby' hoping someone with a 'primary' slot would not show up. Maybe, just maybe, they could get that vacant slot.

An Instructor appeared and addressed the crowd. He said there were only thirty slots available. He would call out the names of those soldiers selected. Three of us were standing there in our Black Berets. The Instructor asked us if we had come back from Panama. We said we had just gotten off the plane and had come back early only because the Regiment 'needed' these slots. He pointed over his shoulder at the classroom and told us to go in and have a seat at a desk. We were in!

Pathfinder School was a challenging and rewarding experience. The mission of a Pathfinder team is to infiltrate into hostile territory and set up the landing zones for large numbers of helicopters that would follow in a main assault force. The team motto was "First in. Last Out."

We studied hard to learn the maximum load of aircraft, the tensile strength of rigging straps, chains and clevises, setup of drop zones, helicopter landing sites and zones, air traffic control, and the proper techniques for rigging equipment and vehicles for sling loading. We set up our helicopter landing zones, rigged our vehicles and bundles, directed in the aircraft, used hand and arms signals to maneuver helicopters into position, hooked our rigging to his cargo hook, and watched our equipment fly away. On one occasion, we set up our helicopter landing zone at night. A helicopter came in, loaded us up and flew us over the zone to see what our work looked like from the air. It was a fantastic learning environment.

There were soldiers from the 101st Airborne, 82nd Airborne, Engineers from Fort Leonard Wood, Airborne School Instructors, and of course, three Rangers. It was a great group of guys. After the days work was done, we would sit around a fire sharing stories and experiences. This was male bonding at its finest. Every school has a historical twist or quirk. This school's tradition was for every student to sample the famous Pathfinder Burger from the Trade Winds Cafe in Cusseta, Georgia. It was a log cabin diner in the sticks of Georgia that made one heck of a burger. The Pathfinder Burger was a huge hunk of beef topped with all the fixings. Combined with a pile of French fries, you would be hard pressed to finish the meal.

The Pathfinder Course came down to the final written test. The first half was fill in the blank questions on any information that had been covered in the course. The other half was a drawing of how you would set up a helicopter landing zone with three landing sites within it. This included all lights, marking panels, ground guides and marked off distances. If you failed, you failed the course.

I always hated test situations but forced myself to concentrate and labored through the test. I got to the end feeling fairly confident I had found the correct solution. There was no way to know of course, because there was no limit to the options on how to set up the landing zone. Because of the size restrictions, I only saw one way to make it fit and that was "tight." I went home that night wondering if I had made the grade.

The next day all students were seated in the classroom anxiously waiting to hear their score. As each student heard his passing grade, you could hear the sigh of relief. In the end, only two soldiers from the 101st Airborne did not pass and did not graduate with the class.

*     *     *

U pon graduation, it was back to training the COLT team. By this time we were getting pretty damn good at what we did. The average week would consist of a HALO jump, a movement to a target and an extraction by helicopter. The Company Commander of the Regimental Headquarters was constantly trying to conduct challenging training to keep the young Ranger motivated. Whenever we scheduled training for the team, we would expand it to include the Company.

On one occasion, I coordinated major events involving many other units. One consisted of a 20 kilometer zodiac boat infiltration down the Chattahoochee River to the back side of Leah Field, on the Alabama side of Fort Benning. Three kilometers out we would kick out Scout Swimmers to recon the landing site and then signal the boats forward. We would then cache the boats and move one kilometer to a Pickup Zone (PZ), where at first light we would be picked up by a UH-1H helicopter. Once on board, we were to fly a preplanned 25 mile route to the other side of Fort Benning. After two false insertions, we would rappel into the Landing Zone (LZ) and then move to lase a target to coincide with a station time for a fast mover with a laser guided bomb.

I coordinated the entire event and expanded it to include the Company. The extra manpower from the Company to execute the operation was in turn good for us. During the coordination phase, Hussein and I drove out to where we planned to beach the boats to see if it would work. It was in a backwater of the river with the old bleached trunks of trees sticking up from the surface. As we stood on an old roadbed which disappeared into the murk, I noticed something strange in the water.

"Is that an alligator?" I said.

Hussein, standing next to me, said, "No way."

I picked up a thick branch of driftwood and heaved it out to the dark spot in the water. As soon as that stick hit the water a three-foot alligator jumped from the surface of the water in surprise and then disappeared. "Glad I'm not a Scout Swimmer!" I said, and we both laughed.

We then asked around at the local fishing and bait stores to inquire about alligators and snakes in that backwater. I was assured big gators had been sighted in a swampy area nearby. It wasn't uncommon for gators over ten feet long to be shot in the nearby ponds and rock quarries near Phoenix City, Alabama.

Execution day came and my two boats started out an hour ahead of the rest of the Company to execute our portion of the infiltration. We motored down the river and across a large lake like backwater until we came to the swampy, stumped stretch of water where we would put out the Scout Swimmers. Doug Fenske and Paul Hussein went into the water. For safety's sake we tagged close behind the boats.

We went through the drill of stopping within eyesight of the shoreline and watching for any movement of the enemy. It was training, but it was Ranger training, and you always executed training to specific standards. Standards in all training were essential and highly adhered to.

We silently moved forward, did a sweep of the inside of the wood line and signaled the boats forward with flashes from a red lens flashlight. The boats silently paddled in and we off-loaded the gear, hoisted the zodiac onto our shoulders, and moved it to a streambed inside the wood line. There we covered it with a nylon netting and placed vegetation over it for camouflage. The whole event took only minutes and then the team moved thirty meters inside the forest. We did final equipment checks and prepared for our patrol. As the team prepared to move, a branch was used to sweep away our footprints and any other signs of our landing. We obviously did a good job because after the operation we learned that the boat recovery team could not find our boat even though they knew where to look. The remainder of that operation was unremarkable, but it became the model that we mirrored time and again.

\* \* \*

In June of 1990, I attended the Long Range Surveillance Leader Course (LRSLC) at Fort Benning. Since I was the COLT Team Leader at Regiment, it was decided I should evaluate whether or not the course would be worthwhile for the rest of the team. I wanted to take the whole team through the course together. I figured this way we could hone the Standard Operating Procedures we had already developed and add new ones after an independent evaluation from the Cadre of the school. The problem was the schedule just wouldn't support it. I attended with a team from the Regimental Recon Detachment instead.

The course was held at the 4th Ranger Training Brigade compound at Harmony Church. This was the same compound that had belonged to the 3rd Ranger Battalion until 1988. At that point in time, it had been decided we would move to the main post and the Ranger School would take our compound. It was a very unpopular event for the 3rd Battalion. In the end, the Infantry School was not interested in our list of arguments. I personally believe the decision had been made. The Infantry School wanted that compound and they were going to get it.

The course was specifically tailored to small unit infiltration and reconnaissance techniques. The curriculum involved enemy vehicle and aircraft recognition, movement techniques, parachute jumps, infiltration/exfiltration techniques, radio equipment and antennas, reaction to enemy contact, survival, escape and evasion. Students had to pass a Physical Training evaluation, a 12-mile road march and a 5-mile run. If you passed those events in the first few days, you could continue on with the vehicle recognition phase.

The vehicle recognition class was a major obstacle. For a week we spent entire days in the classroom watching as slide after slide of vehicles flickered on the screen. A slide would show for five seconds, the screen would go blank for two seconds and then the next slide would appear for five seconds. This continued until fifty slides had been viewed.

During the instruction phase, a slide would appear and the instructor would point on the screen with a wand while narrating the characteristics of the vehicle, "This is a Soviet T-55 tank. It is found in a variety of third world countries. Notice the egg shaped turret, five die-cast road wheels and a flash suppresser two-thirds the way down the barrel. This is a Soviet T-55 tank." Then came the next slide and this was continued all day, day after day.

Finally test day arrived. I was ready to identify thirty-five of the fifty slides. The first slide flipped on the screen and all I could see was the top of a vehicle, swimming in water. The next slide flipped up and you could just make out the top of a turret in the bushes. The next slide showed a barrel sticking out of some trees and on and on it went. For a whole week, we had nice clear pictures of these vehicles and on test day it would have been easier to identify the trees and shrubs that hid the equipment. I failed miserably and had to spend the entire night studying. The next day was the retest and I don't know how I did it but I passed. I don't mind saying it was sheer luck, but I passed, and that was all that counted.

To test us further, we broke up into three man teams and were given a map of five stations dispersed over a three-mile course. The teams began at ten minute intervals. The intent was to run to the station, dive behind a spotting scope and attempt to correctly identify a two inch model of a vehicle that lay out in the grass. The best time combined with accuracy of identification made a total score which identified the winning team.

We ran in BDUs (Battle Dress Uniform) and field boots and carried two quarts of water. I outran the other two members of my team and dove behind the scope. I was breathing hard and struggled to see through the sweat that ran into my eyes. I couldn't get a clear view of what was out there. The closest comparison to this drill would be the marksmanship portion of the Pentathlon. I took a deep breath, looked through the scope for a few seconds, and then rolled out of the way so the next team mate could get a look. We agreed on the vehicle, wrote it on the answer sheet and then ran to the next station. In the end, we had the second best run time but did terrible on the identification. It was a tough event but excellent training.

We then conducted movement techniques combined with a live-fire range. This included Quick Fire techniques, where you fired your weapon instinctively to kill someone you happened upon in the woods. Also, a reaction course where the team suppressed a stronger enemy force, threw smoke grenades, and then broke contact. We rehearsed and then executed a variety of techniques to react to enemy contact and then tried them out on the live-fire range. The training was very realistic and we shot a considerable amount of lead downrange. After the patrol broke contact with the enemy, the decision had to be made to move to an extraction site or continue the mission.

Infiltration was by a helicopter parachute jump and the exiting method of choice was the Small Patrol Infiltration and Exfiltration Rig (SPIE) rig. We all received refresher training with the SPIE Rig. The pilots took us on a flight route over Weems Pond to see the two huge alligators that lived there and then returned us to where they had picked us up. To think we actually got paid for this!

The next event was to spend a night in an underground hide site to see if anyone was claustrophobic. It was an underground bunker with no windows or cracks of light from the outside.

Once the hatch was closed we were totally sealed in this hole. It was meant to simulate bunkers that had been built in Germany. When the Soviets rolled by, Long Range Surveillance (LRS) teams would peek out holes in the ground and report enemy troop movement to the Allies. No one freaked out, and the next day we were on to another event.

We had a week long block of instruction on High Frequency radios, radio wave propagation and construction of antennas. Each student was required to figure the proper length of his antennas, then to supervise the construction of the huge thin cable antennas by the team. It wasn't uncommon for one half of the antenna to be fifty feet long but with practice it was no problem to get it up in seconds. Once the antenna was constructed, we would make a radio check with the Mountain Ranger Camp in Dahlonega, Georgia, to see if we did it right. There was no smooth talking your way out of shabby work.

The highlight of the course was the instruction on survival, escape, and evasion. We picked our way through the woods with blindfolds on to simulate the blackest of nights. We learned to make shelters, snares and traps, wild plant identification, preparation for eating and how to build fires with a bow and stick. After we covered how to make a shelter and find food off the land, we transitioned into weapons making and the killing and cooking of animals.

For the course, we had to kill, gut and skin an old billy goat, rabbits, and chickens. These replicated animals we had caught in our traps or had stolen from local farms and villages. Some of the students were disgusted by seeing the billy goat getting his throat slit. I was from the farm and therefore didn't see what the big deal was. A few of the students shook their heads, grumbled, and turned away so they would not have to watch. We learned to break the neck of the rabbit with a quick chop and then squeeze its entrails out of its rear end. We rung the chicken's necks, and then it was time for cooking.

We cooked in a variety of ways including boiling, frying, roasting on a spit, and baking in tinfoil. The point was to be creative and see what turned out. We also used potatoes and onions that had been stolen from the locals. Generally, the food turned out quite good. I hadn't known an old billy goat would have such a strong and greasy meat. I don't know why anyone would eat one by choice.

The course culminated with a series of patrols to perform reconnaissance on targets around Fort Benning. We reconned (reconnoitered) places such as bridges, road intersections and unit compounds. We would move into the area, go into a hide site, and locate a position to observe the objective. The entire time a platoon of OPFOR would beat the brush throughout the day and night looking for us. Twice they came within feet of stepping on us in the bushes but did not discover our hide site.

On one patrol, we had to cross the rain swollen Upatoi Creek. It was raging, but the Instructor was convinced we could cross it. He had made a bet earlier with the other Instructors that he could make it and he intended to try. We reached the creek and walked alongside it until we reached a spot that looked quite wide and was therefore probably shallow. The Instructor stuck his staff in the water feeling for the bottom and waded in. After three or four steps, he was up to his chest. I was a couple of feet away preparing to grab for him if he lost his footing.

I said, "Sergeant, I don't think you really want to do this. It's not safe and it's not worth it. Besides, you're taller than half of us and if you barely make it, we sure as hell won't make it." He thought about it, but didn't like the idea of giving up. "Come on Sergeant, let's either go find a bridge or call it off." He relented and we moved into the woods and built a fire to get warmed up. It was extremely wet and cold and he made the right decision.

The final patrol ended with an escape and evasion exercise. The scenario dictated that we were compromised by the enemy. We were on the run and had to make it to friendly lines without being caught. We ran through the ditches and culverts and never saw an OPFOR. Of course, we didn't want to see one because if we got caught we would be taken back to the start point and made to do it all over again.

The LRSLC was an excellent school taught by extremely experienced and professional instructors. The planning, communications training, live-fire ranges, helicopter movements, parachute jumps, and survival training were exceptional. These were critical skills for small unit operations. They would provide a foundation for our future training at the Regimental COLT.

\* \* \*

After my return from the LRSLC, I immediately turned my attention to planning a grueling exercise that would validate the combat readiness of the team. The mission would consist of a 30 kilometer movement through those same nightmarish mountains along the Tennessee Valley Divide (TVD) culminating at the Mountain Ranger Camp. Along the way we would recon and possibly engage a target with a Laser Guided Bomb (LGB).

After a phone call to the local aviation unit on Fort Benning, I found they would gladly insert us into the mountains. They made routine flights to the mountain Ranger Camp for Airborne training with the students. Next we obtained maps from the Mountain Ranger camp and the planning of the operation hit high gear.

We could use the evaluator frequency of the Ranger instructors for an emergency channel and the OPFOR from the school would serve as our target. The weakness in the event was the actual engaging of a target with a laser-guided bomb. There were no impact areas in the Mountain Ranger Camp so we would have to settle for a simulation of the target being engaged.

On mission day, we loaded the MH-60 Blackhawk helicopters and sat back for the ride to northern Georgia. We flew east of Atlanta and could see Stone Mountain off to the right side. As the terrain started to grow rougher, it was time to get ready to hit the ground. I watched the ground below me and recognized a group of buildings below to be the Mountain Ranger camp that I had been in five years before. We flew the same route I had trudged on my first mission and continued north. As we went, I wondered when the pilot would finally reach the Landing Zone. It was just a little clearing on a mountain top small enough to fit one bird into.

"ONE MINUTE!" Finally we crested a ridge line and the helicopter made a quick landing into a break in the forest canopy. We jumped off each side of the helicopter and hit the dirt as the helicopter rose from the ground and flew away.

The team jumped to their feet and moved into the tree line to conduct a listening halt. We crouched there quietly, listening for the sounds of any enemy coming to investigate and could see the helicopter fly away in the distance. I took a quick look at the map and then called the team into a huddle to tell them the bad news.

As I pointed to the south I said, "Do you see that farthest ridgeline along the horizon? Not the dark one but the faint one you can barely see? We're going on the other side of that!" They looked at me and someone said, "Who the hell scheduled this crap anyway?" Then we all laughed.

The move was incredibly grueling as we moved for three days across mountains, ravines, shallow streams and "dinosaur land." Dinosaur land was a term given to incredibly overgrown and remote pieces of forest where no living thing had probably been since the dinosaurs were here. It was strange, but these were some incredibly thick and musty places in the forest where everything was quiet and nothing moved. Usually, you found dinosaur land along swampy ground and lowlands. Other times, you would encounter these areas unexpectedly on ridgelines and on the mountains. The silence in these places gave you an eerie feeling and made you move a little faster to get out.

We located the enemy "command post" which consisted of a large tent set up in the woods and determined no OPFOR was in the area. We completed our patrol and sent a SITREP to the Regimental Headquarters via satellite communications. On the third day, we reached the mountain Ranger Camp and moved to the Aid Station to have a Medic check the blistered feet of the team. The medic asked what we thought of the Iraqis invading Kuwait.

I asked, "What are you talking about?"

"Yeah, Iraq invaded Kuwait." he said.

I asked, "Where's a phone I can call the Regiment on!"

I went to the Camp Commander's office and he saw me coming. I introduced myself and he directed me to the telephone. The Regimental S-3 answered, and I asked if we needed to get back to the Regiment due to current events. There was a pause on the other end of the line. He then told me to continue with our training and check in every day.

I hung up the phone feeling that we needed to get back to the Headquarters. There was no one there from the Fire Support office if anything did happen. I also knew that Rangers had a bad habit of not recalling people from training when something was up. The Ranger leadership always felt any change in training, or recall of personnel, was a 'red flag' to the news media or spies. Therefore, Rangers routinely were not recalled from schools and other high visibility training before an operation commenced. We did not want to be left behind and I coordinated a military van to transport us back to Fort Benning.

\*        \*        \*

W hen we reached the Regimental Headquarters, we found the staff attempting to gather information and get a handle on what to make of the situation—much like the rest of the world. I played no actual role in the planning of the Ranger missions for Desert Shield or Desert Storm. It was because of my position that I remained updated on incoming sensitive information that flowed into the Regimental Operations center. I also attended all briefings on tentative missions and targeting as units began to deploy to the Southwest Asian Theater.

The mission that the Ranger Regiment would play in a hugely mechanized war was unclear from the beginning. Undoubtedly we would conduct a high risk mission during the initial phases of the attack to oust Iraq from Kuwait. Three major options were identified: a raid on a major Iraqi command bunker, a raid to disable an Iraqi chemical plant, or a raid to secure the American Embassy and hold it until attacking forces relieved us. All three options were considered to be extremely high risk and high casualties were projected. Regardless of the chosen mission, there was no doubt it would be a success. We could infiltrate any area and destroy or kill about anything. However, getting out can be more difficult.

In any of these scenarios, we would be far behind enemy lines. Since we had very limited vehicle capability, there was no way to get out. Even if we could find enough vehicles to hot wire at the target, our only option was to drive west, under friendly air cover and hope to link up with friendly armor units attacking to the east. The casualties could be horrendous.

During first week of August 1990 the order came to prepare to move within the next ten days. It was to be a high profile event so we could tell our families. We wouldn't have to disappear in the middle of the night as was usually the case. They wanted Saddam Hussein to know we were coming to help draw the line in the sand.

The message traffic began to dictate units and the dates they were to deploy. The decision had been made to deploy heavier units than the Regiment and we began to slip farther and farther back in the priority of movement. Finally, it was announced that we wouldn't go to the desert to sit around. Instead, we would move over just before the attack into Kuwait would commence. Training continued at a high pace and we fully expected to receive the call to move at any time.

\*     \*     \*

The EC-130 Talon airplane flew a lonely nap of the earth flight, using every contour of the earth, to stay close enough to the ground to avoid enemy radar contacts. The EC-130 was specially designed C-130 transport plane revamped as an electronic command post. Onboard, in its reduced sized cargo bay, were thirty Airborne Rangers and two Air Force Combat Control Team members. This was the Jump Clearing Team of a Task Force that followed thirty minutes behind.

The moonless skies over this desolate stretch of countryside would only be interrupted by the sounds of airplane engines invisible to anyone on the ground. This corridor of sparsely inhabited land had been carefully planned months before and there was little chance of the enemy watching the skies in this area tonight. Highly publicized maneuvers were taking place hundreds of miles to the north to divert all attention where it could do no damage.

The airplane vibrated and shuddered as the pilot steered around mountains and dropped into valleys enroute to the target. The Air Force Loadmaster looked under the illumination of red lights at the special cargo he was responsible for. They were seated in five rows on the floor, one man in front of the next. They sat between each other's legs so that when the man in front leaned on the man behind him his head would lie on his chest. This was necessary because absolutely no space could be wasted. The thirty Rangers each had a rucksack, weapon, and load bearing equipment with ammunition with him on the floor. Also, each man had a main and reserve parachute strapped to the tailgate, which accounted for all of the space in the aircraft. It never ceased to amaze him how these Rangers could sleep through about anything. Oh, there were the few men awake holding plastic barf bags to the mouth and emptying their stomachs of anything they had eaten lately. That was normal for new arrivals. The mixture of nerves and the stomach butterflies caused by the constant up and down and side to side maneuvering aircraft could tear anyone's stomach up. The rest of them seemed to be oblivious to the world. In another five minutes he would have to wake these "sleeping beauties" so they could in-flight rig their equipment and make final preparations prior to the jump.

*"Navigator has three hours to target,"* announced the navigator through the intercom. *"Roger,"* replied the aircraft Loadmaster. The Loadmaster stood, shook the Ranger primary Jumpmaster on the shoulder, held three fingers in front of his face, and shouted, "Three, hours!"

The Jumpmaster nodded his acknowledgment stood and slapped his hands together. "Three Hours!" could be heard above the roar of the engine. The nearest Rangers acknowledged by echoing the command. Then each man shook the man next to him until all jumpers were awake and struggling to their feet. They had been wedged in this position for three hours already and they shook their limbs to get the blood into the tingling parts of their bodies.

The Loadmaster then unstrapped the parachutes sitting on the ramp. This was the last chance for each Ranger to empty his bladder. A five gallon water jug was passed down the aircraft for each man to piss in. The latrine at the back of the aircraft was blocked with equipment. One buddy held the can and the other buddy relieved himself. As this process continued, the Jumpmaster passed out the parachutes.

They were passed man to man until the man farthest to the nose of the aircraft got his first and then worked to the rear. Once every man had a main and reserve parachute, he worked with a buddy to don his equipment and get it adjusted properly.

Once the team had all equipment on, except their rucksacks, they put on helmets and waited for the Jumpmaster to inspect their rig and gear for deficiencies.

The Jumpmaster stood directly in front of the fifth jumper he would inspect. From experience he knew this would likely be the last jumper he inspected. There were usually enough Jumpmaster qualified Rangers to ensure all jumpers could be JMPI'd in a timely fashion. The aircraft lurched to the left and everyone still standing fought to keep their balance. The Jumpmaster's hands never left his jumper and he blew the running beads of sweat off his nose and upper lip. It wasn't hot in the aircraft. It just took an incredible amount of energy and concentration to inspect jumpers in cramped conditions on a continually lurching and shifting airplane. The Jumpmaster completed hooking the rucksack to this fifth jumper, grabbed his hand, and held on tightly as the jumper lowered himself to the floor. The jumper now had nearly two-hundred pounds of equipment on and sitting down was no more than a controlled crash to the floor. The Jumpmaster looked around and saw that the other four Jumpmasters in the clearing team had completed their task. The Jumpmasters all took a piss before rigging and inspecting each other.

*     *     *

Thirty minutes behind the EC-130, on three C-130 and four C-141 aircraft, were the rest of the main airfield assault force. Two-hundred more Rangers along with more Air Force Combat Control Team members were onboard. All of the personnel on these birds were executing the same mission of rigging to jump as the clearing team. Some Rangers had even greater challenges.

Onboard, these aircraft were also Ranger Special Operations Vehicles. These vehicles were loaded so they were ready to off-load and be immediately put into operation upon the landing of the aircraft. Once the jumpers had their parachutes and equipment on, they sat on the side of the vehicles, all of the way from the left door to the nose of the aircraft. Each man not jumping had a safety rope still tied around his waist and snapped to rings in the floor. Each Ranger would unsnap from the floor as the aircraft touched down at the destination. In case of a crash this was their seatbelt. The only exceptions were the men on the vehicles who were belted into the vehicle and the jumpers themselves who had one big seat belt. It was an A7A cargo strap stretched from one end to the other to ensure the men would stay in one place upon a crash landing.

*   *   *

"One hour!" screamed the Jumpmaster. The jump clearing team was alert and passing over the details of their mission in their heads for the last time. Call signs, check points, and how to hotwire a vehicle as fast as possible. The jump clearing team had a simple mission. Jump and within thirty minutes get all obstacles blocking the airstrip off of the main runway and mark the lead and tail ends with IR lights. This was critical because thirty minutes later the assault force would be attempting to land. The ability to accomplish this mission would lead to the first Decision Point of the night for the Airborne Commander. *Can we land? Or, do we have to drop the rest of the assault force to assist in securing the airfield? Then come around again later to land the aircraft.*

These aircraft were not conducting a drop and then heading off somewhere to refuel. These aircraft would land one behind the other, with no lights, on a blackened out runway. Then the planes would off-load men and equipment and wait for the Rangers to board again. Then in an event driven sequence they would vacate this airfield. Hopefully no one would know who had been there that night. Regardless of how it was accomplished, these aircraft were the ride home. Once the jump commenced for the runway clearing team these aircraft *had* to get on the ground.

*       *       *

One-hundred miles to the east was an enemy military complex that had been under surveillance for the past two weeks. An intercepted communication between the commander of this installation and the commander of another installation far to the north asked whether or not he had safely received his "shipment." He said he had and the intelligence community considered this the clue they had been waiting for. All available Human Intelligence (HUMINT) sources along with aerial photos from satellites confirmed a shipment of containers had arrived and the size and shape of the containers was consistent with the worse case scenario the "Spooks" had warned about for years.

This extremist country had developed and transported a nuclear device to this compound. This county had threatened to use a device such as this on its neighbors or even the United States. The threat was taken seriously enough that the directive was given to prepare a mission to eliminate the possibility.

The President had had tried to use diplomatic channels to gain access to military facilities for inspectors but instead was given a communiqué announcing the death of this country's Prime Minister. Although he had not been a staunch ally of the United States, he was considered the one bit of stability in this volatile situation. The situation was unstable, and therefore the

President decided on action over diplomacy to ensure the safety of U.S. citizens. A limited action to seize the nuclear device and display it for the world to see was authorized.

Eighteen hours later a Joint Service Task Force had assembled and for two days rehearsed a mission to extract the "precious cargo" from enemy control. After those two days, the situation in this small unstable county had not changed and the authorization was given to execute the mission.

Less than an hour from that compound were four CH-53 Pavlo helicopters with auxiliary fuel tanks for extended range flights. These helicopters were capable of inflight refueling and would refuel in the air on the trip home. Onboard these special operations aircraft were sixty U.S. Army Rangers and other "operators." Their mission was to assault the compound, secure the precious cargo (PC), and transport it to the awaiting PC Bird at the airfield, one hundred miles to the west. From there it would be whisked out of the country to safety. The remainder of the force would then exfiltrate.

*   *   *

The airfield seizure would commence fifteen minutes after the raid on the compound to ensure no alert could be sent to the compound. Nothing would be left to chance. Intelligence analysts speculated the device might also be at the airfield and forces at both targets had to be prepared to seize it.

An AC-130 gunship had arrived at the compound fifteen minutes ahead of the assault force. The gunships' mission was to take out any identified guard posts, antiaircraft positions and any armored vehicles it could identify. He also had one other mission—isolate the target and ensure no vehicles entered or exited the target area. His attack on the airfield defenses would coincide with the attack by the raid force on the compound.

Specter had no problem executing this mission. Actually, it was this aircraft's specialty. His IR camera could detect vehicles and personnel, regardless of how they were camouflaged, just from their body or engine heat. Then he could use his choice of its 105mm Howitzer, 40mm Bofor cannon or 20mm cannon to engage the target. His fires would come straight down and could pierce almost any target.

The gunship continued a constant left bank and orbit around the target - all the weapons pointed out the left side of the aircraft. All the while the weapons control officer scanned for the planned targets and other targets of opportunity. *"O.K., I've got two large vehicles at the ends of the runway. Probably ADA, let's get them first,"* he announced. He sat on a chair looking into a monitor in front of him. On the monitor he could clearly see the vehicle and personnel on the ground. It was a simple task to move the crosshairs on the screen over the target with the use of a joystick and then press the red button. With that, the aircraft shook from the 105mm cannon firing and a bright flash, followed by the heat of an explosion, showed on the screen. You couldn't hear it, but the screen told the story.

*       *       *

On the ground, the night had seemed tranquil, as was usually the case. Only the random guard at a very quiet station could hear the slight, constant drone of an aircraft overhead. The crews manning the ZPU-4 anti-aircraft guns on the end of the runway had been trying to decide what kind of aircraft was coming into their airspace but they couldn't see it and it sounded far away. This was a remote and little used airfield and they weren't used to having business this late at night. Then the crew on the south end of the airfield was dead. The crew on the north end had time to spin their quad .50 caliber weapon in a circle one time. They searched for a target—then they were also dead.

The officer in charge had been in the command building which was located next to the barracks. When he heard the explosion, he ran outside to see what was happening. As he exited the building, he was met with a bright flash and as he fell backward to the ground, he saw the barracks explode. As he tried to gain his senses, he felt an instant of heat and then he was dead too.

\*     \*     \*

*"OK, I've destroyed the ADA, barracks, command build and arms room and am now moving to the guard towers,"* announced the weapons control officer. *"Falcon One this is Thumper 53 ... you are cleared on target to drop,"* announced the Specter pilot.

*"Three minutes to target."* announced the Talon pilot.

*"Navigator has twenty minutes to target."*

*"Roger,"* said the Loadmaster. He then flashed twenty minutes with his fingers to the Jumpmaster.

"Twenty ... Minutes!" yelled the Jumpmaster as he extended both arms and held up ten fingers two times. The Rangers were alert, giving each other a thumbs up and a few beat their heads to shake out any cob webs and get their game face on.

"Ten! ... Minutes!"

"Get! ... Ready!

"All Personnel! ...Stand Up!"

The Rangers struggled under the weight of their equipment to get to their feet. Those who managed to stand up in turn helped those who couldn't.

"Hook ... Up!"

"Check ... Static ... Lines!"

"Check Equipment!"

"Sound Off For Equipment Check!"

This was a ramp jump and all jumpers hooked into the left side inboard cable and took a reverse bite (a backhand grasp of ten inches of ripcord) as they held the slack of their static lines.

The Jumpmaster looked forward in the direction of flight, through the crack in the ramp, as he tried to identify the airfield. The loadmaster had just flashed him the sign for three minutes and he needed to get a good look at the airfield. The pilot and navigator would switch on the green light when they thought they were over the target but the Jumpmaster is the double check and it was his responsibility to make sure they were over the right target. If not, he did not let his Rangers jump. On the other hand, he had better be right!

Tonight it was too easy. As the Jumpmaster looked off the side of the ramp he could see the flashes of explosions and the illumination from some small fires helped him to identify the blacked-out airfield. "STAND BY!" This was a tailgate jump, and the Jumpmaster would lead the way. He assumed his position at the front of the stick and focused his attention on the red lights at the end of the ramp. When it turned green, he would step off into the night.

The stick (jump order) had been arrayed so that a fire team would land on each section of the main runway and simultaneously clear it and then move to the taxiways. A CCT was positioned toward the front and rear of the stick, so upon landing they could emplace IR lights on the ends of the runway and a navigational beacon for the aircraft to home in on.

The green light appeared, "Follow Me!" and the Jumpmaster walked off the end of the ramp. As his body was swooshed away by gravity and the wind, his static line ripped open the parachute deployment bag on his back and pulled out his parachute. The parachute immediately filled up with air and slowed his fall with a groin-wrenching stop.

As each jumper left the ramp, his static line remained attached to the aircraft and blew in vicious circles, off the end of the ramp. Each jumper had to be careful to exit off the middle of the ramp or he could be bloodied by the whip of these nylon ropes. On this night there were no apparent problems, and as the Loadmaster watched the trail of parachutes string out behind his aircraft, he began to pull in the static lines and close the ramp. The Talon then assumed an orbit above the target area and continued to jam any enemy radio communications.

In the air each Ranger ensured he had a good canopy above his head and then looked for other jumpers, to make sure they did not become entangled in each other's parachute. Next, they searched the ground below to steer clear of any obstacles and find a "safe" place to land. Many terrible accidents had happened in the past, such as Rangers landing on fence posts, runway lights, wind socks, and buildings. The one place they knew they could land safely was on the concrete. The concrete was unforgiving and any mistake would surely result in a broken bone. The trade-off of knowing you wouldn't have a piece of metal rammed up your ass still made it the landing pad of choice.

One-hundred feet from the ground, after making sure no jumpers were close enough to be entangled, the Rangers lowered their rucksacks to the end of a ten-foot cord. When the jumper heard that rucksack crash to the ground he knew he had about three seconds until impact. The trick was to bend your knees, pull you elbows in tight to your chest and place your hands over the face. Then with a little pressure in the knees allow the upper body to relax. A crash, followed by a bone jarring tumble on the pavement and a brief drag across the rough texture of the concrete by your wind filled parachute, was the best that could be expected. As long as you could clear your head and move all of your body parts it was a success! The jumper then pulled out his weapon, chambered a round and looked for the enemy. He also looked for a fellow Ranger knocked out by the impact and being dragged across the airfield by his parachute. Unfortunately, it happened all the time.

\*       \*       \*

*AH-6 Little-bird in action.*

A hundred miles to the east another Ranger force was looking for something special. "Ropes out!" screamed the Loadmasters on the four Pavlo helicopters. A second gunship had just completed taking out the defenses of the compound and now these birds hovered over the target. The ropes were out and Rangers fast roped from three birds into blocking positions to isolate the target. This ensured no reinforcements could get into the compound and anyone still alive could not stop the securing and loading of the device. At the same time, the fourth bird hovered over the buildings where the containers were known to have been taken. In that same minute, the Ranger clearing team was on the ground. The Rangers isolated this building while a Special Forces clearing team went inside. The Rangers were ready to clear the building themselves if needed.

If the precious cargo was not found in this building, the Rangers were also prepared to clear every building in the compound until it was found. Time was of the essence and the ground commander wanted to be off this target in under an hour. If he could do that, the chance of a reaction force trying to stop him would be slim to none.

\* \* \*

*"Thumper 57 this is Death 3 and 4, we are four minutes from target."* This was the flight lead of two Air Force F-16's approaching the area. The F-16 is a precision air to ground Close Air Support fighter/bomber and his mission tonight was to emplace a Gator Minefield and a major road into the compound. The minefield would be laid three miles out using an aerial delivery bomb. The bomb would be released, fall to a point above the target and expel cluster munitions (bomblet mines) that would then rain down onto the roadway. These bomblets would remain in place until a vehicle ran over one or could be set to self detonate at a time when the raid was over. The task force commander was taking no chance that an organized reaction force could jeopardize his mission.

Specter replied, *"This is Thumper 57... Roger, no ADA threat identified."*

\*   \*   \*

The deafening explosion of the concussion grenade exploding inside the building was followed by the clearing team bursting through the door. This was the standard building clearing stack. First man low and left, second man straight and then right, third main high and left, and fourth man high and right. In seconds the entire room could be scanned and targets eliminated with the pull of a trigger. Triggers were pulled three times and the building secured. As expected, the container was found secured behind a set of metal bars and minutes later the bars were opened with the help of a charge of C-4 explosive.

The four Pavlos had left the target after the insertion had been completed and were laagering two miles to the west. *"This is Team Leader ... Mary!"* the pilot heard in his headset. That was the ground commander telling him to get his bird to the compound and load up the device. A few minutes later he landed on the courtyard in the middle of the compound and seconds later took off with the Precious Cargo and the clearing team and a fire team of Rangers for security. He would fly low and fast and head straight south toward the airfield.

Meanwhile, the blocking positions had started to take sporadic sniper fire and returned fire at will. The night was their ally in situations like this. They could sit in the cover of darkness and identify the enemy through their Night Vision Equipment long before the enemy could see them. If the enemy tried to sneak up through tall grass or vegetation, their body heat could be seen through a PAS-7 thermal scope or MS-46 Stinger Night Sight. It was eerie to look through those devices and see the image of the heat given off by a body. It was like you were looking at his soul. If these advantages weren't enough, they still had the security in the sky—gun ships. As long as they were there, nothing could move and live long enough to be a serious threat.

\*   \*   \*

At the airfield, one-hundred miles to the west, work continued in the blackness of the night. The Bravo Team Leader into his MX radio, *"Charlie 5 this is Charlie 21, Red 3 is clear."* He had just finished clearing another section and hadn't found anything blocking the runway. He continued to run with the other three members of his fire team and his Forward Observer continued to follow a few meters behind. "Specter sees a large vehicle in Red 4!" puffed the FO. "He says it is about two-hundred meters south of us." The team leader only glanced in the FO's direction and picked up the pace even more. Two minutes later, they approached the vehicle. It was an old dump truck parked sideways in the middle of the runway. The fire team approached it slowly carefully and cleared the vehicle without opening the doors. With a flashlight they check in the bed of the bucket, under it and in the windows. Nothing seemed out of the ordinary and they opened the door. Inside there were no keys and another man opened the hood. There was no battery and therefore no way to hotwire it. "Get the brake off and let's push it!" All five Rangers heaved against the monster old truck and it wouldn't move. *"Charlie 21 this is Charlie 09 we need help in Red 4 we've got a big dump truck we have to push off the runway."*

The clearing team leader announced into his radio, *"Black 6 this is Charlie 21, we have a large obstacle in Red 4 you are not clear to land! Estimate 15 minutes to clear obstacle."*

*"This is Black 6, GET THAT OBSTACLE CLEARED ASAP!"* The airborne Commander's worst fear had just come true. He had men on the ground, the runway was blocked and he didn't know for sure he could get the planes on the ground to extract his personnel before and enemy reaction force could get to this airfield. *"This is Red 6, Option One!"* All Chalk leaders answered in order from each of the following transports and acknowledged Option one. The assault force would jump the rest of the Battalion to secure the airfield and clear the runways so the planes could land. The Jumpmaster on each bird echoed those same jump commands which ended with the Jumpmaster in the door looking for the drop zone. "Three minutes!" screamed the loadmaster over the roar of the wind in the open door.

\*   \*   \*

"Push God Damn It!" Bravo Team continued to push for all they were worth and out of the darkness came four more Rangers from Alpha team. "All together ... Heave ... Heave ..." and the old beast started to move. At this time Charle 32 arrived with another five Rangers and the beast gained speed.

*"Red Six this is Charle 21, the obstacle is clear...you are clear to land!"*

\*   \*   \*

"Option 2...Option 2 all aircraft option two!" The loadmaster on each bird grabbed their Jumpmasters and echoed the word that it would be an air-land. The Loadmaster slammed the doors shut and the Rangers on board went into a controlled frenzy. They had three minutes plus a few minutes on the runway to get out of their parachutes and get on their combat equipment. The Rangers on the vehicles and aircraft crew scrambled to help the jumpers get out of their equipment, shove the parachutes into their kit bags and pass them man to man to the nose of the aircraft to be stacked out of the way. Within three minutes all the jumpers had transitioned to the air-land option and had their rucksacks on, weapons at the ready and radios turned on. The cabin went to black out lights and night vision devices were turned on. IR lights in the floor that had been invisible to the naked eye now shined brightly.

The RSOV team drivers were behind the wheel and another Ranger stood by each shackle. After the wheels touched down and the initial slow down two shackles would be broken on the vehicle and after the slowdown the other two would be broken. The ramp would open and immediately upon the aircraft stopping the RSOV's would lead the way off the ramp followed by personnel and then motorcycles. The personnel would immediately turn left or right off the ramp to avoid being run over and continue to their planned positions. The motorcycles would move on planned routes to Observation Posts or to clear taxiways of obstacles. The RSOV's would move on planned routes to blocking positions to prevent any enemy from interfering with operations on the airfield.

The pilots of each airplane flew with night vision goggles toward the blackened airstrip. There were no lights remaining on the entire airfield except IR strobes that had been placed at the lead and tail ends of the runway. These were special operations pilots and this was their specialty. The planes appeared from nowhere because they were also totally without lights. No one could be on the runway, on foot or in a vehicle, because you could not tell if an aircraft was coming until it was already on top of you. Runway crossing points had been established and these were the only places to cross the runway. An Air Force representative was at each point and he would listen to the air traffic control and let Rangers waiting to cross know when to move out. If anyone took it upon himself to cross at any other point, he was literally taking his life into his own hands. Also, if the collision of the airplane with his flesh just happened to damage the bird, it could jeopardize the entire operation.

All vehicles had to move within thirty meters of the runways and taxiways and no personnel could move within thirty meters of the runway thus eliminating the possibility of someone getting run over. It had happened before and the lesson learned the hard way. Vehicle speed was limited to ten miles per hour as a result of other tough lessons learned as vehicles had disappeared into drainage ditches as they drove without lights with the aid of NVGs. Nowhere on this target would you see any light from these late night visitors. It was pitch black, and unless you had the hardware you were blind as a bat. If you had a flashlight, you weren't an invited guest and your chances of surviving more than the next few minutes were drastically reduced!

\*   \*   \*

Whoa ... my head was fuzzy and eyes burning ... I rolled over in my creaky army cot ... *was that a dream?* I reached down and felt the broken bone in my right ankle. Maybe it was ... but I felt like I had just lived it.

# Chapter 5
## The Dark Side

The call to deploy did not come and it was late October. I was quickly coming up on a big decision to make. My long awaited class date for Officer's Candidate School (OCS) was scheduled to begin on November fourth. I did not want to leave if the Regiment did deploy to war. On the other hand, if I turned down the slot and the Regiment did not deploy, there was no telling if I would ever get another chance.

I went to see MAJ Jeffrey Shaeffer, who had taken over for MAJ Newnam, and asked for his "take" on the situation. His position gave him access to the Regimental Commander and I felt he likely had the best information I could access. After some pondering moments, MAJ Shaeffer told me that I should go to the school. He said, "Besides if something does happen, you'll surely get your chance to get to the desert after you are commissioned."

That wasn't really the point to me. I wanted to go to war with my team and the 75th Ranger Regiment. I had a tremendous level of loyalty to that unit and felt I couldn't live with myself if I wasn't in the action with them. It was a tough decision.

Each day I would go to the Secured Communication Information Facility (SCIF) and try to get a feel for any change in the situation. There was none. Finally on the 4 November 1990, I drove myself the four blocks to the Officer's Candidate School. All the way to the door I felt I was making a huge mistake. On my 29th birthday, I left the best job and unit in the world.

\*       \*       \*

Officer's Candidate School (OCS) was a fourteen-week rite of passage to the Officer Corps for all enlisted soldiers. Many states have their own National Guard OCS programs. There was only one Federal OCS program and it was located at Fort Benning.

Most of the candidates came from the enlisted ranks across the Army but some also came from the College Option program. This allowed a college graduate to enlist, attend basic training and move directly into OCS. The downside was these soldiers didn't have a base of practical experience to start with. The upside was the Army gained high quality people fresh out of college.

The cadre of OCS was historically all Officers from different branches and commissioning sources. My class had the dubious honor of having the first set of Drill Sergeants assigned to increase the discipline level of the curriculum.

OCS was a phased course that began with the candidates in a recruit status and increased to candidates with true officer status. Each phase was incremental and revocable based on class performance. My class climbed its way up and down that ladder from week to week.

The next couple of weeks started to form a routine. Daily events consisted of early morning PT, barracks maintenance, chow, classes, chow, study hall, barracks maintenance and then sleep. The only wild card was the daily no notice formations and, you guessed it, grass drills.

Each student was responsible to carry his own weight. Without teamwork it would be impossible to complete all of the tasks at hand. Again, everyone had their strengths. It could be boot polishing, brass shining, making a bed or folding the clothes to fit a display. Whatever the skill, it saved time and made life much more bearable.

Another major time consuming task was to memorize two sheets of famous quotes from past military leaders. There was also the 'saying' and 'quote of the day'. It was impossible to commit them all to memory. Each day in the chow hall on the way to the door you were called before the cadre and asked to quote any of the sayings. If you failed, you got demerits. Demerits were worked off only by marching the sidewalks of the courtyard during visiting hours for families. I never had to march and looked forward to any visits. Meanwhile, outside you could see the perfect marching, much like you picture at the Tomb of the Unknowns, with crisp moves along the edge of the sidewalks.

The classroom curriculum focused on leadership and counseling skills. The tactical and field curriculum was infantry based and focused on field craft, raid and ambush techniques, and land navigation. It was quality training and the candidates learned from each other and specific cadre with individual areas of expertise.

On 7 February 1991, I graduated from OCS. CPT Matt Brown read my oath, my wife pinned on my rank and Doug Fenske, Greg Blackwell and Paul Hussein all attended my graduation. They lined up in a row and said at the same time, "Rangers Lead The Way, sir!" and then saluted. I then flipped the silver dollar traditionally given to the first enlisted soldier to salute a new officer. It went over their heads and landed on the ground. They had to fight over it and I cannot remember who won the battle.

After almost six years I finally left Fort Benning and made the long trip back to Fort Sill, Oklahoma with the whole family in the front of a Ryder truck. It was a long drive, but we pushed on through the night and arrived early in the morning.

\*　　\*　　\*

The Artillery Officer Basic Course had a reputation of being quite difficult because of the gunnery solutions that had to be computed to accurately place artillery rounds on the target. It involved physics, weapons characteristics, ballistics and a large quantity of computations involving formulas and slide rules. None of this was my cup of tea to say the least. It started out auspiciously as I failed my first test on propellant and projectile nomenclatures. Gradually I gained confidence with the material and managed to get through the gunnery portion of the course. The rest of the course dealt with tactics and fire support which was the strength of my personal experience.

One day I came home at lunch to find my wife completely broken up. My brother-in-law Bill Owens was in the Marine Corp and had deployed to Desert Storm. She had gotten a call from her mother that said he had been hurt. No other details were available.

It turned out that he had gone on a recon patrol with his Reconnaissance Team to scout the mine fields that the Corps would have to breach to enter Kuwait. Upon returning from the patrol, his team was turning in their grenades and ammunition when a guy next to him somehow pulled the pin of a grenade. The resulting explosion killed the guy and severely damaged Bill's leg. A MEDEVAC had been called, and they thought they had lost him on the bird, but they managed to keep him alive until they reached the Field Hospital. He survived, but the damage was so severe he had to leave the Marine Corps and transition back to civilian life.

Two other major events took place during this same time. Two Battalion Commanders from the Ranger Regiment died in a helicopter crash into the Great Salt Lake in Utah during

Special Operations training. Apparently, the weather was bad. As the helicopter crossed the lake in heavy rain and winds, it went down killing everyone but the pilot. The pilot said he did not want to fly the mission in that type of weather but felt pressured to do so due to the intensity of the training. Onboard was Harvey Moore an acquaintance of mine. It was another case of a small community, a very hazardous profession, and the loss of another friend.

My brother-in-law, Dave Owens, was in the 1st Ranger Battalion, and called to let me know what had happened. He was quite unsettled by the whole event. I told him it was a terrible situation but unfortunately, the nature of the business. As time went by, he would see a number of friends come and go. If you did your job right and didn't make any stupid mistakes, it was a matter of destiny. You would be one of the lucky or unlucky. I also told him he could take heart in the fact that only so many Rangers die in training. If he hadn't already been counted as one of the unlucky ones, chances were destiny was on his side.

The other major event was the crash of two buses carrying Rangers from the 3rd Battalion to and from a live fire range on Fort Benning. The two buses collided head-on killing at least one officer and injuring a number of other soldiers. A friend of mine, still in the Regiment, called to let me know what had happened. After learning an officer had died, I was on the telephone in minutes.

I had been trying during the entire class to work an immediate return to the Ranger Regiment should a slot open up. I wanted to let them know I was available. As I dialed the phone, my wife looked at me like I was crazy, inhuman, and totally insensitive! I looked back and said, "What?" This is the way it is—this is the business I'm in. If a comrade falls, another has to step up and carry on with the mission. It's the nature of the profession. Unfortunately, there was no opportunity opening up for me. I would have to carry on with my unfortunate plans to join the "mech" world.

The course ground on, but sooner than I would have expected, it was over. I finished the course and was relieved to know I would continue to have a job for at least the next four years. For me the course had been easy. I was glad to get to Fort Carson and see if I had any chance to see the desert.

\*　　\*　　\*

In May of 1991, I graduated the Field Artillery Officer Basic Course and immediately moved to Fort Carson, Colorado. It was a bittersweet move because the entire time I was at Fort Sill, I had continued to try and work a deal to return to the Ranger Regiment as a Fire Support Officer. The Regiment was more than happy to have me, but not until I had spent a year somewhere else. I was pissed off, but actually agreed that seeing the "regular" Army was the best thing for me.

Colorado Springs is a beautiful city nestled under the heights of the Rocky Mountains. Pike's Peak and Cheyenne Mountain towered above the city. Cheyenne Mountain was the location of the North American Aerospace Defense Command (NORAD). This was the U.S. military command center to counter an incoming nuclear missile threat to North America. Fort Carson sprawled out across the plain directly below. North of town was the Air Force Academy. Falcon Air Force Base (renamed to Shriever AFB in 1998) sat to the east. Peterson AFB also shared the Colorado Springs Airport. Colorado Springs was a very progressive and military oriented city. The scenery alone made it a wonderful place to live.

It took a couple days to settle the family. I then reported to the 3/29 Field Artillery Battalion Personnel Officer (S-1). The 3/29 Field Artillery of the 4th Infantry Division (Mechanized) was a unit famous for not being on the cutting edge and actually on the back burner for modern equipment fielding or real world deployment plans. The 4th ID had the mission to be prepared to deploy to any theater in the world, though it rarely did. One thing that the 4th ID excelled at was deploying to and fighting at the National Training Center (NTC) in Fort Irwin, California.

That was no small accomplishment as NTC is the armored unit equivalent of Joint Readiness Training Center (JRTC) and fought on the wide open and deserted expanse of the Mojave Desert. Many units got their butts kicked at NTC. If the 4th ID could win there regularly, that meant there was something very good about this unit.

This would be my first experience with a mechanized unit and its soldiers that I had badmouthed for years. My stereotyped expectation was fat, lazy and unprofessional troublemakers doing the utmost minimum to collect a paycheck. Many said it is easy to be a leader in a Ranger Battalion where the soldiers are the cream of the crop and extremely motivated, but the true test of a leader comes when he tries to lead and motivate the less than ambitious.

A completely different leadership style would be necessary. These soldiers were not used to being cussed at and physically motivated and actually would not stand for it. Yes, this was the "kinder and gentler" volunteer army. If you were too aggressive as a leader, it was almost guaranteed that a complaint would be lodged against you. The quick rule of thumb would be to treat each and every soldier with respect, step back and make maximum use of your patience.

I was assigned to Alpha Battery as a Fire Direction Officer. The first guy I ran into was CPT Joe Adams. Joe was an energetic and happy guy who was always game for a competitive event like running, mountain biking, wrestling, etcetera. He was of Filipino descent so he wasn't a big guy but he was scrappy. Joe was also one of my Company Fire Support Officers in 3rd Ranger Battalion and now my Battery Commander in the 4th ID. He had made a name for himself as the Battalion Fire Direction Officer at the last NTC rotation by calling fires on himself as his position was overrun.

As a Fire Direction Officer I would calculate and then provide the appropriate firing data to the howitzers to launch rounds accurately downrange. This was a whole new world for me and I did not look forward to starting this job.

I walked into the Battery to meet the Officers and First Sergeant. They immediately asked if I would be willing to deploy in two weeks to REFORGER (Return of Forces to Germany). We would fly over, pull equipment out of the pre-positioned warehouses (POMCUS sites), drive them around and then do maintenance on them. POMCUS sites were large warehouses of American armored vehicles stored and maintained in Europe so in time of war only troops had to be transported. The time and cost savings to redeploy to Europe was significant. I said that I'd love to go and packed my bags that night.

Around three-hundred of us from the Battalion loaded a chartered plane and began the long trip to Germany. We landed in Amsterdam, loaded buses, and drove past the windmills and dikes toward Germany. We crossed the border and passed into the gate of an American compound nestled in the forest. The compound was alive with hundreds of troops deployed from the U.S.. The soldiers were housed in massive circus tents while other tents were set up for amusement areas and chow.

Over the next few days, we completed our mission and then explored the countryside. We took a series of bus tours to various famous battlefields to include the bridge at Remagen, Verdun, Bastogne and the city of Cologne. The depth of history in these places was mind boggling. You could see the skeleton of an ancient knight with a hole in his forehead or you could visit a museum of the more modern wars. One thing I discovered on that trip and still carry with me today is my taste for *Hefeweizen* beer. It is a strong beer with yeast that accumulates on the bottom of the bottle. You poured the upper two-thirds into a glass, swirled the yeast on the bottom of the bottle and then poured that into the glass too. It is excellent.

We returned from Germany and I began my new job in earnest. In June of 1992, the 3rd Brigade of the 4th Infantry Division deployed to the National Training Center (NTC) at Fort Irwin, California, and 3/29 Field Artillery deployed as its Direct Support Artillery. Major (MAJ) Patrick, the Brigade Fire Support Officer, and Lieutenant Colonel (LTC) Guy Borne had a concept they wanted to try out in this battle. LTC Bourne called me to his office. He said he wanted me to run his single brigade COLT and gave me a free hand to roam the battlefield making as much trouble for the enemy as possible. I would be the trump card.

I told him I was experienced with COLT operations. To make it work I would need infiltration and exfiltration corridors, communications to talk long range, a HUMMWV instead of an armored Fire Support Team Vehicle (FIST-V), a dedicated battery to do voice communication Call for Fires and the leeway to move by myself. He told me to contact Major Patrick for anything I needed. He was anxious to see how we would do.

I met with MAJ Patrick and discussed my concept of the operation. His only reservation was that I would have to take his HUMMWV, which produced a good laugh. Next, I met with my new COLT members. The Team Sergeant was SGT Dustin Jones, was a husky guy with an extreme amount of technical competence but had not really been challenged to this point. The other two members were Fire Support Specialists. Both were in their twenties, cocky, and like SGT Jones, still untested. Five days after I met them, they competed in and won the DivArty Best FIST Competition. That meant they were very good at their jobs and we could start our preparation for NTC at a fast pace.

We had a free hand to conduct any training necessary and worked out of the back gate of the motor pool for the next month. This was some of the best quality training I had ever experienced in fire support. We practiced intensive mounted and dismounted navigation, infiltration and hide site techniques, proficiency training with the laser target designator, engaging a moving target at various speeds with real vehicles, and how to plan for and execute Copperhead (laser guided artillery rounds). We trained as a team, but ensured each individual could complete the mission. The focus was on enemy order of battle, vehicle identification and threat, enemy equipment and its limitations. The team was ready to meet the best Opposing Forces (OPFOR) in the world in the Mojave Desert.

The last week in June, I departed with the advanced party. We would prepare to receive the main body of the Battalion that would arrive the next week. Meanwhile, the Battalion loaded their equipment onto trains and then traveled via bus to meet the equipment again at Fort Irwin.

My group arrived in the desert early in the morning. The familiar landscape of rocky hills and mountains, sandy flats and sparse vegetation seemed to go on forever. The bus unloaded us at a set of sun shades referred to as the Dust Bowl. This was a fitting name as the sun baked it unmercifully, and when the wind blew through the area it picked up and carried the dust along.

The sun shades were no more than pavilion type roofs on stilts that gave the soldiers a place to get out of the direct heat of the sun when they were not working. There were a few other buildings and trailers which contained some video games and telephones for people to call home. All in all, these were very austere living conditions.

Around 2 a.m. on the third night, I awoke to a loud rumbling noise in the distance. I assumed an armored column was rolling by at a very close range. As the sound grew louder, I felt the ground tremble and then shake violently. The metal supports of the sun shades creaked and clanged together. It was an earthquake. Most of us sat up to take it in. It lasted about a minute and then faded away.

The next morning we listened to the news on the radio. It reported that a very large earthquake had taken place with the epicenter about fifty miles from us. We went to breakfast inside a dining facility. While we were eating, pictures on the walls started shaking and silverware and glasses rattled due to an aftershock. A female cook fled from the kitchen and screamed as she ran outside. Periodic aftershocks continued for the next few days and then faded away.

The new Battalion Commander, LTC David White, arrived the next day. I was assigned to be his guide and driver. I met him outside the Star Wars building early in the morning and he smiled and shook my hand. LTC White was about six feet tall and had a medium build. He was also very friendly and personable. Over the next two days he was very interested to hear my observations about the status of the Battalion. We talked often as we drove over the entire expanse of NTC. It was the equivalent of four-wheeling and getting paid for it. We would grind our way to the top of the highest peaks we could reach with the HUMMWV (which can go about anywhere) and take in the rugged beauty of the valleys stretched out below.

The next week the Battalion's main body arrived. Their first week was spent downloading equipment off the railhead and drawing other equipment from the motor pools at NTC. All vehicles were uploaded with equipment and personnel and prepared for combat. The Battle Staffs prepared the scheme of maneuver for the first battle. I would be attached to the 82nd Airborne which had sent a Battalion to augment the 4th ID.

I conducted coordination with the 82nd ABN S-3. The S-3 turned out to be MAJ Snukis, the burly and aggressive tempered Lieutenant I had known from the 3rd Ranger Battalion. Their Battalion Commander, LTC David Barno, had been in the

Ranger Regimental Headquarters when I was a Private in RIP. I conducted my coordination, and during a rock drill, briefed the assembled leaders on my part in the scheme of the maneuver.

The first mission would be a defense of the Whale Gap with the 82nd positioned forward and the 3rd Brigade of the 4th ID defending in depth. It was my intent to reach the top of the Whale (a small whale shaped mountain) just before the enemy armor advanced and engage targets with Copperhead laser guided artillery rounds as they moved toward us.

All night an infantry battle raged on the Whale. Just before dawn I requested permission to move into position. The Infantry Commander on the Whale gave his permission and we rammed our HUMMWV up an incline with no roads to avoid being ambushed.

We got into position, set up our equipment, called our artillery battery and found out no artillery would be in position until an hour later. We watched forty enemy armored vehicles roll straight down the road where we had planned to engage them and into our defenses. We were in the right place, had good communications and had the enemy in our sights. The only problem was we had no artillery.

All we could do was give situation reports and watch them come. We tried to call for the 105mm artillery from the 82nd but they told us to get off the radio. Our part in the first battle amounted to nothing. The OPFOR broke through and continued past us on the valley floor below. We let them go and drove off the mountain in the direction they had come from and exfiltrated without problems.

Over the next two weeks, we conducted seven battles across the mountains and valleys of NTC. My COLT team moved around the battlefield raising hell as ordered. We sneaked, crawled, climbed, charged, cleared bunkers, breached obstacles and gave the enemy a hell of a headache.

On one occasion, a tank Battalion was defending forward and enemy BMPs (Soviet block armored infantry personnel carriers) threatened its Tactical Command Center. MAJ Patrick sent me forward with my COLT to assist. When we arrived, we found we were positioned inside the bowl of three big hills with the BMPs running around outside the bowl. I went outside, grabbed the team and climbed to a rock outcropping to look across the valley floor. In the next hour, we killed three enemy BMPs and eliminated the threat. A year later, that Company Commander was at Fort Carson still telling stories about that being the damnedest thing he had ever seen.

In another action on the Whale, it was my COLTs' mission to infiltrate onto the Whale to provide intelligence and Copperhead fires supporting the Brigade attack. The brigade would move to the north to retake the valley and attack into the central corridor on the other side. We knew the enemy would have a counter reconnaissance screen line established. We used a series of unorthodox measures to slip past them undetected.

We used the same method of slowly rolling forward while providing security in all directions with our night vision goggles. We pulled out the thermal night sight from the Ground Vehicular Laser Locator Designator (G/VLLD). We used that to pick up the enemy vehicles with hot engines to our front and pick a route around them. We sneaked past a couple of enemy vehicles, but when we rolled out of a slight depression, we were face to face with a BMP at about fifty yards.

I announced, "Plan B!" The vehicle stopped and a Specialist and I jumped off the vehicle. We reached in the back cargo area and grabbed two prepared rucksacks which held our laser, radio and Rangefinder. We then dove into the scrub brush to conceal ourselves. The vehicle then sped off to draw attention away from us, and went into its role as a retransmission station.

The Specialist and I then crawled on our hands and knees all the way around that damned BMP for about a hundred meters. The gravel and stickers from the plants cut into our hands and knees. Finally, we were behind them and marched for over twenty kilometers to the Whale. In the daylight, that mountain looked very large. At night while walking toward it for hours, it loomed bigger and bigger. The entire Whale was about four kilometers long and two kilometers at its widest point. All of the edges were steep. On the map it looked like it was formed with a cookie cutter. When we reached the eastern end of the Whale, we encountered a steep rocky incline. We began to climb up the rock walls of an almost vertical cut in the mountain. If we could get over the steep portion, we knew there would be a flatter sloping area on top.

I lied a few times to the Specialist and an Observer Controller who made the climb with us. I was out ahead and scouted for the easiest path. After I crested a knoll I would say, "Hey, we're over the top! Come on." After a while it got kind of funny. That was the type of energy you fed off of during a grueling task like this. We continued to push and got over the top before daylight.

After a short search we found a small depression amongst the rock and established our hide site under a camouflaged net. We pulled out our radio, established communication, and waited for daylight. As the morning gray grew lighter we saw the whole battle unfolding below us. The artillery had changed positions so we did not have the laser angle to utilize Copperhead. Therefore, we called mission after mission of conventional munitions. We suppressed the enemy while providing current intelligence during the attack.

On another occasion, we sneaked past an enemy Observation Post, a BRDM (Soviet block wheeled armored scout vehicle), a BMP, breached a tank ditch and concertina wire on foot, cleared a trench line of sleeping National Guardsmen, killed two more BMPs and a T-55 tank, and suppressed enemy trench lines with artillery. In an unorthodox move, we fired Copperhead artillery rounds at two HIND-D helicopters on the ground. Because of this action we successfully led the enemy commander to believe that the Brigade's attack would come through this valley. He repositioned forces to repel the suspected attack, but our main effort actually went through another route.

Our COLT team was a great success and we received accolades from the Observer Controllers. They said that we were a major success for the Brigade because we knew our equipment, how to infiltrate and get out, and how to use the tactics required to fight in this environment. In the end, we tallied twelve Copperhead kills, two high explosive kills, an unknown quantity of infantry casualties, and had suppressed enemy positions during all of the last six battles. Those artillery kills accounted for over half of the vehicles killed by fire support in the entire Brigade for the rotation. We were also labeled the only reliable deep intelligence source for the Brigade during the entire rotation.

\*      \*      \*

U pon returning from NTC, I assumed duties as the 2-35 Armor Battalion Fire Support Officer and then the 3rd Brigade Targeting Officer. I learned a great deal about staff planning and Tactical Operations Center operations in both of these jobs. I also learned a true respect for the killing capabilities of the M1 Abrams and the Bradley fighting vehicles. I had long talks about leadership philosophy with my Tank Company Commander as I doubled as the Battalion Fire Support Officer. Looking back, the experience was invaluable. I was a light-fighter and this time in the mechanized world had widened my horizons.

During my time at Fort Carson, I learned much about the regular army and about myself. This had been my first look at the soldiers of the Mechanized Army. I had worked with some fantastic people and some that were very average. The Officers were professional, motivated, and everything you would expect. The NCOs were a mix of good and bad. Personal work ethic and where they had been 'raised' in the army set the NCOs apart from each other. The soldiers were a mixture of highly motivated individuals and some social duds. Many had no desire other than to treat their service as 0600 to 1700 job. Others were making their time go by as easily as possible to collect their college money and get out of the Army.

Both of these attitudes irritated me to no end! Military service required every individual to work to the limits of their ability, as a team, to help the unit achieve its full potential and complete its mission. Lazy and/or unmotivated soldiers at all levels threatened the mission and bad attitudes can bring down an entire unit's morale. I remember trying to explain to a driver from the inner-city of Miami that as long as he was in the Army he should try to do the best job possible. When he collected his college money, he could look back at this service and be proud of what he had accomplished. He looked at me like I was smoking 'whacky weed'! He explained that he understood the minimum standards the Army required. He would do exactly what it took to get by and nothing more. He angered me so much I thought I was going to have to hurt him!

During my two years at Fort Carson, I had spent an incredible amount of time in the field with both the 1st and 3rd Brigades as each assisted the other to train-up for NTC rotations. This created an incredible amount of stress on my family and home life. Consequently, my marriage began to fall apart. My long hours combined with the stress of trying to do a stellar job at work drove a wedge between us. We couldn't seem to communicate about anything. When I got home from work, all I wanted to do was spend time with the family. My wife wanted to get out of the house. We needed to find a happy medium, but looking back, we never did.

This situation was not unique to me. Oddly enough I had counseled many soldiers on their marital problems while not even being able to identify how serious my own problems were. Military service is incredibly hard on families. Many families are not able to survive the long periods of separation. That separation allows the couple to grow in different directions and lose that special bond. In my case, it was even worse. I was a hard charger and a perfectionist who loved what he was doing. I spent long hours at work after everyone else had left in order to complete my projects. During family time, I was a workout Nazi. I was attacking my job just as hard as I had when I was single. Now that I was married I was having a hard time maintaining my work standards while providing time to be at home. The happy medium was very hard to find.

Meanwhile, I was 'chomping at the bit' to return to the Rangers and Special Operations which is what I thought real soldiering was all about. I just couldn't be happy in the mechanized Army knowing the Ranger Battalions were preparing to meet a threat somewhere in the world. I knew that action in Haiti would come soon. It had been a briefed hot spot for years. In the history of the U.S. military, a major action took place every five years: Vietnam, Grenada, Iran, Beirut, Panama, Kuwait, Somalia, Afghanistan, and Iraq. Haiti was on the horizon.

I secured a slot in the 2nd Ranger Battalion at Fort Lewis about eight months out from a projected reporting date and began training in earnest to arrive in the best possible shape. I had run and lifted weights consistently since I arrived at Fort Carson and they remained my strong points. My major concern was the twelve-mile road march in the stifling heat of Georgia in July. I would be coming from the arid and comfortable climate of the mountains knowing fully well how brutal Georgia humidity could be. My buddy, Bruce Carswell, was going to the same Ranger Orientation Program (ROP) class. Bruce was a big guy around six foot two inches tall and two-hundred and twenty pounds. He was always happy, funny, and people enjoyed being around him. To get into shape we road marched diligently during the heat of the day during lunch hours and on the weekends. We worked hard, intent on leaving nothing to chance when we arrived at Fort Benning.

My wife seemed to be very supportive of the move and actually wanted to get a change of scenery herself. She knew I couldn't be happy doing what I was doing. Perhaps a change of scenery would brighten my attitude. In retrospect, she said she wasn't even sure she would make the trip to Fort Lewis with me. In the end we decided to move the entire family to the Northwest. After working out for months, Bruce and I departed Fort Carson late in June of 1993 for ROP at Fort Benning, Georgia.

# Chapter 6
## Back In The Game

Bruce and I took three days to make the drive from Colorado to Georgia. Our plan was not to wear ourselves out before we arrived. During each stop, we took care to work out and run in order to acclimate to the humidity across the plains. Bruce and I held the same philosophy that it was all work and no play until we completed this series of physical tests which were our ticket to bigger and better things.

We arrived at Fort Benning and checked in at the Ranger Orientation Program (ROP) desk to receive our schedule for the next two weeks. I knew many people and the surroundings were as familiar as when I had left two years earlier. The attitude of the cadre was very interesting. It consisted of, "Yeah, we know you did big things the last time you were here, but what have you done lately? Do you still have what it takes?" They had seen more than their share of old Rangers attempt to come back into the Regiment and fail the physical standards required to get back in. For me it made it even more of a challenge to prove I still had what it took to be effective.

During the first couple of days we conducted the Physical Fitness Test, swim test, five-mile run and some Ranger Standards classes. Around the third day it was time for the twelve-mile road march which we knew was the major obstacle to success. The event would start at midnight to minimize the effects of the Georgia summer. Unfortunately, there is little difference between a sticky Georgia day and a sticky Georgia night—especially if you just came from the mountains.

At the command of "GO" we had three hours to complete the route around Lawson Army Airfield arriving at the finish line looking fresh enough to engage in a battle if required. Bruce and I ran as a buddy team for the first two miles and gained a ten-minute advantage. We then settled into a run/walk pattern that carried us to the halfway point. I don't mind saying that the heat really kicked my butt. At the halfway mark I was totally drenched in sweat from head to toe. There was no question that we would keep going, but I was truly concerned that the heat might get us. Bruce was doing better at the turn-around point which was strange, because during all of our training I had generally been the stronger marcher.

On the six to nine mile stretch, we would run three telephone poles and walk one. At nine miles, I actually started to feel better. At ten miles we could see the lights which led up the road to the finish line. At that point, there was a new surge of energy but the problem was we both ran out of water. Then at ten miles, Bruce's left rucksack strap broke and this road march was starting to become a bigger chore than it had to be. We pushed hard uphill the last mile to the finish line, and when we crossed it, I was one relieved and happy camper. That was the only event that could have stood in our way and we had passed it in good shape.

The remainder of the course consisted of land navigation, giving each other IVs and conducting two static line jumps. Each Ranger had to be proficient in administering IVs because during training and real world situations no one knew who would have to play the medic. Cross-training was essential.

After a small graduation ceremony and a few celebratory beers, Bruce and I stopped to visit Doug at his apartment in Columbus and hang out for a few hours. Then we made the trip back to Fort Carson and continued on to Fort Lewis.

\*  \*  \*

I arrived at Fort Lewis, Washington, in mid-July and signed into C-Company, 2<sup>nd</sup> Ranger Battalion. My family would arrive a week later and I needed to find an apartment to rent. For the next few days I worked in the unit and when my family showed up and I still didn't have a place rented. This created some stress because I would be deploying to Fort Bliss, Texas a week later. Finally, we settled for a small apartment, and I prepared to deploy.

*2/75 Ranger Battalion jump; Mount Ranier in the background.*

When we arrived at Fort Bliss, it was obvious major assets had been committed to this operation. The Regiment had assembled and we all felt that something was in the air. A-Company from 3/75 Ranger Battalion had departed for Fort Bragg. My Company, C-Company 2/75 Ranger Battalion, had been placed on alert. No one seemed to know what was up and we continued executing Joint Service Special Operations training for two weeks. The Company that had deployed to Fort Bragg later returned to Fort Bliss. They had no sooner unloaded their gear when they reloaded the bird and departed again for Fort Bragg.

*DAP engaging targets with a .50 caliber machinegun.*

That was when we learned that Company from 3/75 Ranger Battalion would deploy to Somalia. My Company from 2/75 Ranger Battalion would relieve them when we assumed the priority alert posture one month later. With training completed we returned to Fort Lewis to await the call to deploy.

The next month it was time for us to rotate into Somalia. Then the word came that a decision was made to leave the Company from 3/75 in Somalia for continuity. The command did not want to receive and orient a new unit on the ground. Therefore, we stayed home and 3/75 Ranger Battalion fought the battle of Mogadishu. It was supposed to be my Company from 2/75 Ranger Battalion but the politicians made us stay home.

Most people would say we were lucky to not be there for the battle of Mogadishu. When you are a U.S. Army Ranger, training to meet and destroy any enemy, you can feel nothing but slighted for having the mission taken away. Maybe some of us would have died in that same engagement, but now we will never know. We watched the same footage as the rest of the country of our comrades' bodies being dragged through the streets and disgusting mobs displaying them like trophies. It was heart wrenching.

When the reports came into the Battalion, we all assumed that we would be deployed to Somalia to avenge our Ranger losses and give the Somalis the 'pay back' they deserved. Only the politicians stepped back from this issue. There was no lack of resolve on the part of the Ranger community and we were prepared to complete the mission. Instead, the mission was scrubbed and everyone came home. What a sickening sequence of events to standby and witness!

There was an incredible amount of speculation and second-guessing by politicians, civilians and people outside the Special Operations community as to why the Rangers would stay on the ground to guard the downed aircraft and jeopardize themselves in the process. Inside the community itself there was no debate. It was an understood bond of trust between all of the special services who worked together in this hazardous calling.

There would never be a set of circumstances where it would be too dangerous for our comrades to come to our aid. One of us would never be left behind or stranded without support to be taken prisoner. We depended on each other and would live or die as a team. It was understood that when the Rangers had trouble on the ground, the attack helicopters would be there no matter how bad it got. Those same pilots knew that when they ran into trouble or were shot down, the Rangers would be there to assist—just like that day in Mogadishu when the helicopters went down. The Rangers reacted immediately to secure the helicopter and the crew. Throughout that night the attack helicopter pilots weathered a hail of ground fire to provide close support to the Rangers on the ground. The situation in Mogadishu demonstrated that no member of the team would save themselves at the expense of any other member of the team. It was a pact drawn in blood.

\* \* \*

During September of 1993, 2nd Ranger Battalion was training in the South Rainier training area on Fort Lewis. I was in charge of running some OPFOR vehicles for the infantry to ambush. One evening I could hear a weak radio call from the Ranger base. I thought I heard them say we were to immediately redeploy to base. I had the base repeat the order three times. We had been alerted and were to move as quickly as possible back to garrison. I contacted the Company Commander who was located with the Infantry Platoons in the wood line and relayed the information. Two hours later we were in garrison and learned we had been told to prepare for movement to the east coast and the invasion of Haiti.

In hours, the equipment was palletized and the Battalion ready as we waited for word to move to the airfield. We waited for the next two days. During that time we planned and rehearsed the mission to seize an airfield somewhere inside Haiti. Detailed planning and rehearsal had been completed and it was time to move. The order to move to the East Coast never came and the Battalion stood down. We eliminated all signs of the operation while directing the entire Battalion to forget that we even talked about it—another aborted mission.

*     *     *

In February 1994, 2/75 Ranger Battalion deployed to the new JRTC located at Fort Polk, Louisiana. We would again do battle with the OPFOR of JRTC and again we wouldn't be disappointed with the unrealistic advantage that OPFOR has at the training center. The Observer Controllers (OC) went out of their way to assure us the playing field would be level. We knew better than to listen to that baloney! We underwent a series of briefings within the Company from previous lessons learned at JRTC rotations. Many of us had a great amount of information to brief. We were clear as to what to expect. Ranger Battalions don't have conventional rotations at JRTC. They conducted Special Operations missions and then exfiltrated to prepare for the next mission. The scenario was driven much like we would have expected to see in the real world.

We deployed to JRTC and rotated directly into the first raid. We infiltrated into a series of blocking positions to isolate the objective that Bravo Company was attacking. Our blocking position was attacked by seven OPFOR—only seven. We heard nothing but some sporadic gunfire from the enemy as we fired back with our laser fitted weapons. We all wore MILES gear, which is a set of laser-activated harnesses activated by being shot by a laser-mounted weapon. The sound of a blank being fired by the weapon activates the laser and then it becomes much like laser tag. It is illegal to hot-rig the laser to fire without shooting and therefore impossible to be shot if you couldn't hear anything. Well, we weren't hearing much shooting but we started to die like flies. Seven OPFOR killed our entire position before another Squad of Rangers came and finished them off.

It was shades of the past and we were totally pissed off. We couldn't use realistic tactics and win here. You had to play laser tag. Stand behind trees and disregard the normal capabilities of your weapons to rip into a target. Again, the Command said it was time to play to win. We started taking it to the OPFOR whenever we could and we inflicted as much pain on them as they could muster on us.

The grand finale was a movement to contact to locate and destroy a military stronghold. As we moved forward, our lead elements ran into the Observation Posts (OPs) of the camp. A firefight ensued and we moved forward. I was the Company FSO and very proficient at calling for fire support. I could call any asset and work several assets at any time. That is exactly what I did. The Company Commander was killed; the First Sergeant got killed; and then the Company Executive Officer moved forward and was killed. Then I called on the Company Command Net telling Platoon Leaders to hold what they had and I would lay a ring of steel around us. I also told the reserve if they were going to do any good, they better get here now.

I simultaneously called in Naval Gunfire, two sets of Company mortars, and Close Air Support. I also called the snipers and said, "You've got two minutes to haul ass or you'll get an air strike on you head!"

"Who is this?" they said.

"This is Charlie 56, move your ass!"

"We're moving!" they said.

I had so many missions going, and on four different nets, that the Fire Markers couldn't possibly keep up. Fire Markers were guys on small four wheelers. They listened on the radio to the grid of the mission. Then drove there and threw out artillery or smoke simulator. If there were any "players" in the area they would assess casualties with a master laser. This laser was called the "God Gun."

If this had been real, there wouldn't have been any enemy left fighting. But this wasn't real and they were killing very effectively all over again. A fire marker drove up and threw a simulator on top of one of our positions saying we had committed fratricide. I screamed back, "Bullshit!" and my OC had to pull me off to the side. I had a Plugger Global Positioning System that showed the exact grid. That guy had pulled up on a trail and just threw the simulator. It didn't matter what I said now, I had killed some of our own guys. The reserve came forward and the battle wound to a halt. I had to make a statement as to why I had killed our own troops. The next morning in front of God and everybody, in a full blown review of the battle, I had to listen to an inaccurate and tailored account of what I done.

When it was over, we had a Company review with our OC. He looked me in the eye and said it was the most awesome demonstration of fire support he had seen in his fourteen JRTC rotations. He said he couldn't believe how I could control so many assets, so quickly, and on four different radios. "Amazing!" he said.

The next morning we had a Battalion formation. My name was called out to move to the Awards formation. I received an Army Commendation Medal for that engagement. It was a vote of confidence and faith by my Commander to let me know he did not give a damn what had been said. We didn't have much faith in JRTC and their games.

\*     \*     \*

In April of 1994, C-Company of 2/75 Ranger Battalion deployed to Eglin Air force Base, Florida for an exercise that would lay the groundwork for the invasion of Haiti. All of the major components of the Special Operations community were present and immediately it looked like this could be something big. Anytime that many valuable assets were assembled on the same airfield it was very possible that the decision had been made to commit forces. Again, everywhere I looked there were people from the past—Doug Fenske, Dave Owens, Greg Blackwell and a host of familiar faces.

The Joint Special Operations community assembled to plan, coordinate, and rehearse the raids. We were to secure and destroy key targets across the nation of Haiti prior to the arrival of the 82nd Airborne and 10th Mountain Division Task Forces. This would be "Operation Restore Democracy."

CPT Parks, my Company Commander, and I were the only two planners in the Company who knew what was officially happening. Because of our Top Secret clearances we planned the mission in detail while the rest of the Rangers were to believe we were doing standard training. It was that ridiculous, but the official line was that nothing out of the ordinary was happening. CPT Parks was a big man at about six feet three, with wide shoulders but more lanky and sinewy than bulky. He was confident and focused on his mission, and I enjoyed having the opportunity to work for him.

CPT Parks and I wrote and coordinated the maneuver and Fire Support plans for the raid on the Heavy Weapons Compound located at Camp d' Application. It called for a Company-sized Air Assault raid launched from Guantanamo Bay, Cuba, preceded by preparation fires from the AC-130 gunships and attack helicopters. We would face four-hundred of the Haitians most dedicated and capable soldiers inside a very large compound. The mission was for us to destroy these forces and especially their armored vehicles to ensure they could not interfere with the operations in Puerto Prince.

The magnitude of this rehearsal was huge. Our timing had to coincide with the timing of operations all across the country. This included planning flight routes to bypass any population centers. It was a challenge to formulate a plan that prevented people from hearing our inbound aircraft, over great distances. We had to prevent any premature alerting of the enemy on our targets. The Company would be carried by six CH-53 Special Operations helicopters escorted by two DAP attack helicopters for in-flight security. We would do an aerial refuel over water and then continue the flight route into Camp d'Application. The entire operation was replicated off the coast of Florida and on a compound built on a remote part of Eglin Air Force Base.

Difficulties in the timing for aerial refueling, command and control communications and in flight considerations were identified on the first night. We adjusted aircraft infiltration routes and adjusted the aircraft timing of all assets to ensure we did not tip our hand. A particular concern was that the Air force CH-53 PAVLO helicopters were extremely unreliable.

Off the coast of Florida, a PAVLO pilot called saying that he was having mechanical problems and was "going down." We found out later he had 'limped' to shore and made a safe landing. It seemed that at least two or three of the birds would be down every time we tried to fly. The Air Force assured us that these birds would be ready and in wartime would fly regardless.

The operation of loading the aircraft was a challenge in itself. It had been determined that a soldier with all his gear on would sink in the water even if he had his B-7 life preserver on. We knew this since a Ranger had put his gear on, deployed his inflatable life preserver, jumped in the pool and sank. The answer was to take off all our gear and place it at our feet. When we went feet dry over the coast of Haiti, we had ten minutes to get the gear back on and be ready to arrive at the target. It was a challenge. We would practice this drill by taping off a simulated cargo area of the helicopter on the ground, load the fake aircraft, take off our gear and wait for the command to throw it back on. Teamwork was everything.

It is very difficult to put on the body armor by yourself. In the dark of night, the difficulties increased. We rehearsed until we got it right and it was no longer a problem.

We executed the whole operation in a second iteration to iron out all previous problems. Everything went well and it seemed we had a solid plan for our part in the invasion of Haiti.

At the same time C-Company went down to Florida, A-Company went to Virginia to do joint training with the *USS America*. The idea was to use aircraft carriers to project light infantry to troubled spots around the world. The ship removed some crew and naval aircraft and replaced it with Army infantry and Special Operations aircraft.

A-Company spent a month on the carrier writing and testing the operating procedures that would be the cornerstone for future operations like this. They were berthed with the standard marine and naval personnel and left their gear in the aircraft hangar decks. The gear was left packed with live ammunition and weapons and ready to be used at the shortest notice. The crew would alert the Rangers who would then scramble to the hangar decks, don their equipment and move to the flight deck. At the same time, the Special Operations aircraft would be warming up and the Rangers would load.

The entire concept was practiced, fine tuned and practiced again until the SOPs were as efficient as could be expected. This culminated in a fly-away live fire raid to the mainland where the validation of the concept was completed. The Special Operations community was prepared to project a large force using a naval flight platform.

\*     \*     \*

In June of 1994, C-Company 2/75 Ranger Battalion loaded a C-141 Starlifter and began the long flight to France for the 50th Anniversary D-day Commemoration. We were to travel to Point Du Hoc and conduct a large number of reenactments and ceremonies to support the international event. We would escort the WWII Ranger Veterans as they revisited the battlefield where they had fought fifty years before.

We arrived in France and quickly moved into a gymnasium where we would live for the next ten days. Immediately we began exploring the countryside and surrounding area by running in our black Ranger sweats. The town's people loved it. "American Commandos!" they would cheer as we ran through the streets of this small French town. It was a special greeting from these friendly people.

The Veterans finally arrived en masse with a touring group. They moved from local celebration to local celebration and, of course, the 'young' Rangers had to accompany them every where they went. I can honestly say that it was one of the most moving and gratifying experiences of my military career to have had the honor to accompany these great men.

These were the amazing warriors that had assaulted the beaches of Normandy and climbed the cliffs of Point Du Hoc to silence the German artillery that commanded the landing beaches from that vantage point. They relived their experiences and shared their stories of success and tragedy as we retraced the battlefield. It made us proud to be American Rangers.

The *Stars and Stripes Newspaper* became the enemy of the trip for some unknown reason. Reporters were taking quotes completely out of context. We refused to answer any questions as they hounded us around the monuments. One news story was particular disturbing. It quoted a Military Policeman (MP) as saying, "There's no way you could make me assault these beaches!" Then the story went on to say that the American Army couldn't execute that mission as the veterans had done 50 years ago. They said soldiers today are much softer, had a different set of values, and therefore wouldn't make the sacrifice.

That newspaper disgraced American servicemen everywhere, and we were particularly offended. SSG Troy Nattress, my Fire Support Sergeant, and I confronted the MP Officer-In-Charge at the Point Du Hoc monument and asked to see the MP Sergeant who had made the quote. The MP hemmed and hawed and finally said that the sergeant was unavailable and had been misquoted anyway. Maybe, but even if he didn't mean it, he should have kept quiet.

On D-Day the Rangers supported a variety of events. The first was the arrival of President Clinton to give a speech to the throngs of people who had arrived. As dawn broke, it was a rainy, cold and blustery day. As we looked out, we could see five or six warships off the coast and it was an impressive sight. I tried to imagine what it must have looked like to see hundreds of ships spread across the horizon.

President Clinton arrived and walked through the Ranger cordon. He moved in, gave a speech and then shook the veteran's hands as he moved to his awaiting caravan of vehicles. This caravan took him the few miles over to Omaha Beach where he did his famous reflective walk on the beach.

They actually cordoned off the whole beach to make room for him to be filmed making a cross with stones on the beach. Of course, those stones had to be hauled in because there weren't any on the beach. Because of that little fiasco, some of the veterans never had the time to retrace their steps from D-Day 1944. They had to remain with their tour groups and would never get the chance. We had static displays of equipment and weapons. Civilians from all countries could step up and handle or inspect the gear. Everyone from little children and women to historical military clubs dressed in old uniforms swarmed around our displays.

We also conducted a reenactment of the climbing of the cliffs. Two of the Ranger veterans actually climbed down and then back up the cliff to the top. The cliff itself was a formidable obstacle. The first thirty feet were completely vertical and the rest of the way to the top was extremely slippery and steep. Old Nazi fighting positions and bunkers are still there with some of the old wire that rimmed the top of the cliff.

*C-Company, 2$^{nd}$ Ranger Battalion at Point du Hoc, France.*

It would have been a difficult task to climb those wet and muddy ropes as machine gun fire and grenades rained down on you from above. The recounted stories told how the first Rangers reached the top and crouched in a shell crater. As one

Ranger peeked over the lip of the crater, he spotted a German crouching right on the other side in another crater. The Ranger quickly rose, killed the German, and the fighting continued in small groups as more and more Rangers reached the top. The fighting continued across five-hundred meters of cratered and barren land to the road which paralleled the beach. To this point, no artillery pieces had been found, so First Sergeant (1SG) Glen Lammel and a small patrol went across the road to the east to look for any clues.

It turned out that due to the Naval and Air Force bombing of Point du Hoc, the Germans had moved the pieces to a small grove of trees. The guns now set about a half-mile inland from the cliffs. 1SG Lammel and his patrol found the guns unguarded. Apparently, the officer in charge of the guns had his men formed a short distance from the guns for a pep talk. 1SG Lammel then threw thermite grenades down the tubes and put them out of action.

About this time the Germans counter-attacked and the Rangers were pushed back from the road but held against the advancing German infantry. One veteran reminisced how he sat in one position. As fast as he could shoot one German, another would rise up. One after another they would fall. This continued until seven German soldiers had fallen in a small group. In the end, the Rangers held their ground until reinforcements arrived and had participated in one of the most heroic and daring actions of any war.

\*     \*     \*

We redeployed to Fort Lewis and again resumed an intense training regimen throughout the spring and summer. The fire support sections deployed to Fort Campbell, Kentucky, to practice control of attack helicopter fires. The infantry spent long hours in the fire house and ranges launching a lot of steel down range. The ammunition and flight hour limitations of conventional units did not apply to this Special Operations community. More munitions were sent down range in one week than many units received in a fiscal year allocation. That was a reality and not an exaggeration.

Each day CPT Parks and I discussed the plan or coordinated for small changes as the plan was continually fine-tuned. The news coverage was incredibly easy to read. We referred to little diplomatic events as "gates" that we had to get through. At the end of the "gates" was the point where the President would commit his forces. These were easy to read and the same in any crisis. They dealt with social unrest, diplomatic efforts, and military activity.

Diplomatic efforts also began to fall into place. The mandate by the Organization of American States was to take action and the commitment of a token Latin American force. Last minute delegations of congressman and social leaders, like Jesse Jackson, traveled to Haiti trying to achieve a break through with a stalling regime. The United Nations endorsed or assumed a 'hands off' posture and allowed the Latin American states to do what they deemed was necessary.

Military activity included a number of events. The commitment of naval forces within sight of the coast was to lull the defenses into a false sense of security as they grew accustomed to activity off the coast. Radio broadcasts were beamed into the country each night to win the minds of the people and let them know the world was watching. The turning back of the boat people by the Coast Guard sent the message that Haitians had to stay and fix their own problems at home.

This was the culmination of the "gates" that paved the road to intervention in Haiti. They set the tone for the public's perception of events in the Third World and human rights groups worldwide called for immediate action. It could be argued that the news media kept our military in business by stirring up public sentiment, which in turn forced the politicians to commit the military as the policemen of the world. Right or wrong, that's how it was.

We continued to train through the summer as these gates were passed and waited for the 'phone call.' I was a CNN junkie and would constantly focus on the television when discussion of Haiti was on. I knew it was near and I was constantly a little edgy. I couldn't really go anywhere all summer. I had to be at the unit at Alert Hour plus one hour. By the time I got the phone call, I would have to be in a meeting in fifty minutes. That didn't leave me much leeway on places to go with the family. Again, it was another added stress on the home life.

My parents came to visit and I had an early morning conversation with my Dad. He always had a feel for what was going on in the world and he asked if I'd be going down south. I said I didn't know but there was rarely a game the Rangers didn't get invited to. I told him I wasn't concerned about deploying anywhere and of the possibility of being killed. My major concern was that if I didn't come home my daughter would get a chance to stay close with our side of the family, to see her cousins and know where her Dad had come from. My father said he was getting older and wouldn't really be able to affect that, but he would let the clan know to make it happen.

Finally, on Saturday the phone rang, "Sir, you are to report to the Battalion Headquarters as soon as possible." Since I wasn't sure I'd be back I gave my family a big group hug and headed for the door. When I arrived at Headquarters, I immediately moved to the briefing room where the staff had assembled. MAJ Cole, the acting Battalion Commander, arrived and the briefing began.

"Gentlemen, we have received the order to move the Battalion to the east coast and prepare for the invasion of Haiti. The Regiment has left the N-Hour Sequence to our discretion."

The briefing continued with the time table for the dispatching of Liaison Officers (LNO), advanced parties and the flight schedule. The S-2 Intelligence Officer, briefed updates to the enemy situation and then the Battalion Commander spoke. He asked his usual series of clarifying questions and then decided to let the men have one last night at home. "Call the alert on Sunday morning."

I returned home and we took the family out to dinner. It was a tense situation and my wife knew what was up. Things had just started to get better and I was about to take off again. It was an emotional roller coaster but it was the nature of the beast. Sunday morning the telephone rang and the voice said, *"Sir, this is a Bravo notification. We are assembling."*

When I arrived at the Battalion, we again went through the normal series of briefings, palletizing of equipment and final preparations of gear. These *no notice* deployments had become routine and we were prepared to move in short fashion. What made this deployment unique was that the Battalion was moving in two different directions: A-Company to Virginia to rendezvous with the *USS America;* B and C-Companies were on their way to Hunter Army Airfield, in Georgia.

On a sunny day in September, the Battalion formed one last time around a PT platform in the compound quadrangle. COL

Cole climbed onto the stand and addressed the men, "Rangers we're ready to move. It's time to do what we are trained for. We will complete our mission and Rangers I promise you—we will bring each and every one of you home!" He raised a clinched fist and paced back and forth. "I promise you that! We will bring everyone home!"

We then moved to our separate areas and loaded the cattle cars and buses for the movement to McCord Air Force Base. From there, we made the familiar six-hour flight to the Initial Staging Base (ISB) at Hunter Army Airfield and moved into circus tents outside of Saber Hall.

At the first opportunity, I moved over to the Regimental tent to find Doug Fenske. Sure enough there he was with several other Rangers I had met through the years. We caught up on family and friends and talked about the upcoming mission. "Check out my equipment." Doug said. He commenced to show me his Car-15 with M203, his 9mm Berretta, his flip up NVGs and a host of special toys and gadgets.

I exclaimed in a questioning tone, "Damn Doug, don't forget you're gonna have to carry all of that!"

He smiled back and said, "I'm not leaving anything to chance." Doug would fly into the palace and embassy area and expected to have some stiff resistance there.

The next week was spent on a variety of activities as the *USS America* finished loading and steamed toward Haiti. We spent a lot of time on the ranges around Fort Stewart confirming the zero of our weapons and bore sighting the Night Vision Scopes and Aim-1D rifle sights.

I also spent hours with my team around a model of Camp d'Application ensuring every Ranger could complete the mission even if he were the only Forward Observer to make it to the ground. We had to prepare for the worst case scenario. That scenario involved the leadership being shot down en route or killed on the ground and the lowest man had to be ready to take charge. Each FO and RTO briefed the Fire Support and maneuver plan from start to finish until I was confident each man had it down. We then sat in front of a flight simulator and watched a computer simulation of the flight into the objective, what it looked like from the air and what we could expect to see for landmarks in the area. We compared that simulated flight to aerial and satellite photos and knew the ground like the back of our hands.

We loaded C-141's and flew to the Forward Staging Base (FSB), Guantanamo Bay, Cuba (GTMO). The flight into the base is unique because you approach land from the east toward a runway sitting just off the beach running north and south. When the plane hits the beach, it does a hard bank to the north and then drops down to the runway. If it overshoots its approach during the turn, it will be over Cuban airspace and the Cuban guard posts will try to shoot it down. The two Ranger Companies downloaded the gear and moved to a tent city for the next two days. We conducted static loading rehearsals on the aircraft and ran through final brief back rehearsal after rehearsal. In each brief back rehearsal every key leader briefed back the key details of the operation. The Special Operations aircraft arrived to include CH-53D Pavlo cargo long range cargo helicopters, AH-6 Little Birds, MH-60 Direct Action Platforms (DAP) and other gun ships. As the air crews arrived, we prepared a detailed model of the objective called a terrain model for the final Joint Services rehearsal.

The crews from all of the aircraft, both Army and Air Force, surrounded the terrain model of the objective and received an intensive briefing on the Ranger scheme of maneuver and what we expected them do for us. Finally, LTC Cole stood and addressed the flight crews. "Gentlemen, I want you to know we have the utmost faith in you, since we have worked together and

I am totally impressed and confident in your ability to get us to the objective. You get us on the ground and we'll do the rest!"

The group broke up and we marshaled for the final loading of the aircraft. As we marched to the waiting aircraft about five-hundred meters away, you had to be impressed with the fire power we were bringing with us: ground mounted M2 Browning .50 caliber, MK 19 Grenade Launchers and Anti-Tank weapons, demolition teams, sniper teams, and highly motivated infantry specifically trained and outfitted for this mission.

Marine and Navy personnel from the base stopped to watch us move to the aircraft and a small crowd waved at us as we moved down the road to the airstrip. We formed into chalk order (each aircraft is a chalk) along side our aircraft and waited to load. The turbines of all the aircraft started to turn and the AC-130 gunships began to take off to our front. Our game faces were on. Tiger striped camouflage paint on the hands and faces, body armor that will stop a 7.62 caliber round to the chest. Everyone moved with serious focus on the mission at hand.

We knew that Jimmy Carter was in Port-au-Prince and we just wanted him to get the hell out of the way. I had packed a walkman down to the air strip to try and pick up news updates on the negotiations. Rangers near me began to question Jimmy Carters' safety, "Shouldn't he be gone by now? Maybe he's a hostage." It did not make any military sense that he was still in the way.

The politicians were telling the Haitian Junta their time was running short. In fact, they were telling their military, "Get ready, get ready, because here we come!" It may seem the intelligent thing to do as a politician, but as a Commander in Chief, if we actually had to execute 'Operation Restore

Democracy', how many lives would be lost due to the lack of surprise? Was that considered an acceptable loss?

Ten minutes from load time, a Loadmaster came out and said it had just come over the radio to "Abort Mission." Carter had made a breakthrough, and the Junta had agreed to step down.

Special Operations gunships were already "tweaking" their guns on fifty gallon drums in the ocean and had to be called back. The 82nd Airborne was in the air outside of Fayetteville North Carolina and were turned around. The flight deck of the *USS America* was alive with aircraft loading and taking off to conduct their raids. We were a few minutes from loading plus a short flight from our objective.

We looked at each other and had one thing to say: "Damn it!" All of the preparation, rehearsal, painstaking planning and training were for nothing. It was not easy to psyche yourself up with the intensity required of the situation and then just turn it off. I was personally devastated and totally disheartened.

It was announced the next day that we would remain in GTMO as a reaction force to snuff out any resistance that might pop up across the country. We created a system of rotating alert companies on a two-hour string and the remainder of us relaxed a little bit. The days to follow were long and tedious. We had freedom to roam this remote part of the base and swim in a large tide pool in the ocean. In fact, it was like a health club with good sleep, a gym, good food, and miles of trails to run.

No one cared—we just wanted to do the mission we came for. Now it looked like we might not even see the 'rock' we had talked about for years. I was so pissed off and had a lot of time on my hands so I wrote a little poem about my frustration.

## "Abort Mission" ... Again!

*We traveled six days to a far away land.*
*Lush covered mountains surrounded by sand.*
*A nation in turmoil, people suppressed.*
*Militants versus poor, social unrest.*

*Not soldiers of fortune who fight for some gain.*
*Professional soldiers, who meet the enemy, seize terrain.*
*We're military icons moved on maps and chalk boards.*
*The President's finest, his political whores.*

*We fight for our nation, family and creed,*
*Savor our victories, watch our fallen men bleed.*
*Trained to be lethal, to devastate, and to kill.*
*Then, "No don't. Just stop! Feed the enemy. Treat the ill."*
*"They are no longer your enemy. They now are your friend*
*This scenario gets played again and again.*

*Talk when you must, barter and trade.*
*Only call on your soldiers when the decision's been made.*
*When the country is threatened, it's people in danger,*
*Then call on your finest, the American Ranger.*

**20 Sept. 94**
**In the Caribbean**

This simple poem reflected the frustration I was feeling. It was definitely the wrong attitude for an officer to have. Therefore, I just showed it to a few friends. As an officer and professional soldier, it was my duty to execute the policies of the President regardless of my personal feelings and that was exactly what I would always do. As long as I kept my feelings to myself, it did not mean I had to agree with the politics of war.

A few days later CPT Parks sent a runner to find me at the gym. I ran back to his tent and he said to get my gear on because we were going into Haiti in a half-hour. We needed to conduct coordination's with some Special Forces (SF) Teams in case we were called to reinforce their positions. I thought he was joking and just looked at him. "Hurry up, we've got to go!" Five minutes later I was dressed and ready to roll.

We boarded a UH-60 Blackhawk with our coordination team. We had two Air Force Combat Control Team members, a Navy SEAL and a Regimental Liaison Officer. Before loading I stood alongside the SEAL and sized him up; I wondered if I could "take" him. He was at least six foot four and two-hundred-forty pounds. He peered at me through his dark Oakley sunglasses and leaned over. I said, "You know, you're a big bastard ... I can still take you!" After a dramatic pause he stood upright, tapped himself on the chest and said with a smile, "Body Armor, it's my body armor." He was a cool guy.

We took off from GTMO and flew for about forty-five minutes across the water to Haiti. I had a huge sense of self-gratification when the mountains of Haiti appeared in the distance. I was finally going to see that "rock." Years of preparation and we would finally get ashore.

As we neared land, the Island of Hispaniola just looked beautiful - deep blue/green water with white sand beaches. Palm trees and majestic mountains rose from the waters edge to make a picture of a tropical paradise. We paralleled the coast and you could see the grass and tin huts of fishing communities. Then we approached our first city. I don't remember the name now but it sat right on the coast and had a fertilizer terminal as its major industry. We hovered over the town and then descended into a local soccer stadium where children began to scamper into the grandstands.

To us this was hostile territory. We locked and loaded our weapons as we neared the ground then jumped off and pulled security to the nose and tail of the bird. The Door Gunners could shoot straight out the sides of the aircraft so that area was secure. The front and rear were the vulnerable areas and we took no chances.

Minutes after landing, a huge crowd of local people boiled into the stadium. Most were happy and waving but we continuously panned the crowd looking for young men with sullen faces and jewelry. Jewelry was a sign of status amongst these people and to have it you needed money. To have money, you had to be aligned with the old government or trading in something illegal. Lessons had been learned in Somalia and we were careful not to let our guard down.

A few minutes later the SF team arrived with a vehicle. We left security with the bird and rode through the street of the town to the local police station. The streets were just big enough for the vehicle to move through and we felt extremely vulnerable as we went. I sat on the right side of the open truck bed and pulled security on the left side of the truck. The man on the other side did exactly the opposite. One thing was clear—if someone wanted to snipe at us, he could do it and get away easily.

At the compound we found the SF Team in a local police station. The Haitian police were milling around and an SF Captain came out to greet us. He took us inside and said that he had no real problem in the area. The local people were denouncing the Junta.

We quickly talked over the extraction plan for his team if troubles did arise. We mapped the primary and alternate route he would take to get to an extraction Pick-up Zone (PZ), his radio frequency and link up procedures in case we had to come in and get them out of the compound. After all questions were answered, we moved back to the helicopter and took off to the next town.

*Conducting coordination in Haiti.*

We arrived at the next town and flew over it for about ten minutes with no sign of an SF Team. If they were there, they were to pop a smoke grenade to show us where to land. There was no smoke and the helicopter made larger and larger circles as we tried to locate them.

Finally, about a half-mile outside of town we spotted a HUMMWV parked along side a river bank. Again there was no sign of anyone. We circled it twice and saw nothing. Our helicopter then moved in to land on a sandbar in the middle of the river. As we neared the ground, I chambered a round and disconnected my safety line, to be able to lean out the door for any potential shot. The SEAL held the back of my LBE in case the helicopter made any sudden jerks.

When the wheels touched down, I jumped off the bird and splashed across the river to the far side to ensure we wouldn't be ambushed from that angle. The rest of the team fanned out on the other side of the river, pulled security and approached the vehicle.

I crested the ten-foot riverbank and walked about ten yards into the woods to a small footpath. About ten seconds later, a group of a half-dozen Haitian men emerged from a wood line about forty yards away. They were dressed in shorts and collared shirts stained with sweat. Each of them carried a machete and moved single file toward me on the trail. I shouldered my CAR-15, pointed it directly at them, and didn't say a word. They did not see me at first and moved to within twenty meters. The lead man then stopped, looked directly at me, got big wide eyes, took a couple of steps backward, and then turned and pushed into the group of men behind him. They all panicked and ran back into the tree line. They were probably farmers coming from their field to see what the commotion was—you could never be sure.

The rest of the team had inspected the vehicle and found it unlocked with no sign of the drivers. The Door Gunner on the helicopter waved us back and we boarded the bird for takeoff. We took off and flew back over the town and smoke streamed up from a clearing in the center of town. We immediately landed and again moved into the compound where the team was staying.

The team commander said he had sent two soldiers to inspect the water treatment plant for the town and had no idea why they weren't near their vehicle. We listened to the story we were hearing and nothing was adding up. We looked at each other and hit the point where it was understood to stop asking questions. The matter was dropped. We completed our coordination, and then left for Guantanamo Bay, Cuba (GTMO).

As our bird cleared the coast and headed out over water, I took a long and hard look at Haiti. I didn't know if I would see it again and I wanted to remember what it looked like. A few minutes out to sea I could see a large ship in the distance. As we drew closer, I could see it was an aircraft carrier and we were headed straight for it.

Someone had gotten his wires crossed and instead of taking us back to GTMO, this aircraft was landing on the *USS America*. The Regimental Command Center was on the America and we were headed there to conduct a debriefing of what we had seen that day. We circled the ship in a holding pattern and awaited our turn to land. Finally, it was our turn and we put it down alongside the big 68 painted on the bridge.

As we stepped off the bird, a guide met us and took us down two flights of stairs to the hangar deck of the ship. He led us over to neat formations of preloaded gear belonging to the Rangers on the ship. All that was needed was for an alert to be sounded. The Rangers would fall in and be ready in minutes to load the awaiting helicopters. We dropped our gear and headed for the Ranger Command Center.

It was a maze of passageways that finally ended at the door to our Tactical Operations Center (TOC). Inside was the same myriad of familiar faces of men I had met over the years time and time again. We were quickly seated in a set of chairs and over the next few minutes discussed what we had learned that day. As soon as we adjourned, I headed off to find Dave Owens, my brother-in-law, to do a little catching up.

I walked though the door to Dave's room and his jaw about hit the floor. We shook hands and caught up on what was going on at home and with the mission at hand. With that completed, he showed me where to sleep. I took a shower and hit the rack. It had been an eventful day that I was so damned greatful to have experienced. I felt that I had at least had the opportunity to see the country and that was all I could hope for at this point.

The next day we were briefed one last time and I had a few hours to load the bird before the return trip to GTMO. I wound through corridor after corridor of the huge ship and was totally amazed at the immensity of it. It was a small city right here on one boat and it was a strange place for a "ground pounder" to wander. Finally, it was time to go, and I said goodbye to Dave one last time and then loaded the bird for the trip back to Cuba.

About a week later, it was reported that a Special Forces Sergeant had been shot in the city of Les Cayes, Haiti. Apparently, he had gone outside at night, inside a police compound, to use the restroom. As he emerged from the outhouse he saw two Haitians sneaking toward the building. He fired his 9mm Beretta pistol in their direction and was sure he had hit someone. He in turn was hit in the outside of the abdominal area missing his vital organs.

The Command then alerted the reaction force. B-Company was the alert element that week and late one evening they got the call to deploy. They threw on their gear and walked down to the waiting aircraft. A short flight later they landed in a clearing around two-hundred meters from the police compound. The compound resembled a religious Mission from an old spaghetti western. Five rust colored, stucco type buildings surrounded by a six to eight foot fence. In the rear was a prison with eight cells.

They immediately set up security on the exterior wall and prepared to conduct raids around the area to root out the men who shot the SF Sergeant. For the next six days A and B-Companies conducted a series of raids which netted a large quantity of weapons, drugs, money and two human skulls. The

Battalion Surgeon inspected the skulls and determined that one belonged to a female in her twenties. He guessed she had been dead for about six months. The other belonged to a young girl dead about thirty days.

*Patrolling the streets of Les Cayes, Haiti.*

The Haitians were big believers in Voodoo and the skulls had come from a reputed Voodoo Chieftain. Because of their superstitions, we continued to paint our faces whenever we were visible to the public. We were told never to smile or wave to the crowd. The Command wanted the people to know that we were there for one reason and that was to kick butt. The locals feared us because we painted our faces, only moved around at night, and appeared from nowhere during the raids. They called us "Voodoo Warriors."

Our turn to rotate into Les Cayes finally came and we landed on the same clearing that the others had. As I moved off the

Landing Zone, I was met by CPT Ed Reinfurt. He shook my hand and said, "Dave, there's nothing much going on here. Staff Sergeant Gardner knows the Fire Support plan and he's at the compound." Ed then moved to load the aircraft for the ride to the Health Club, and I moved with the Company to the Police Station.

We arrived at the Station, established security and made a plan for patrolling the city at night. At the same time we also considered possible targets for upcoming raids and analyzed tips received from the local people. The first night we moved through the city without incident to set up a roadblock in vicinity of the waterfront. This was a location where boats could load and unload goods into the many warehouses along the wharf. It had been reported that there was a large cache of weapons in one of those warehouses and we were hoping to get lucky.

Each night the gunships flew continuously overhead to give us reports of civilian movement around our positions as we moved. Nothing could move without being seen through their infrared cameras. They would report moving vehicles, crowds of people and paid special attention to the rooftops.

When we reached the warehouses, we found the main intersection and melted into the shadows to wait around for a while. As we waited, a man approached our position and before we could stop him, he slipped into a warehouse. We pursued him to the door and it slammed in our faces. The large metal doors were backed by metal bars much like you would find in a prison. We couldn't get in without a blow torch. I could see through a crack in the metal doors well enough to see it was some type of woodshop. Along the back wall I could see the guy moving in the background.

*Voodoo Warrior in front of emptied jail cells.*

We had brought our translator along with us. Jean was an Air Force Academy student whose parents had emigrated from Haiti. He had been in the Academy at Colorado Springs when he was yanked out of school and put on active duty for the duration of the invasion. Jean had initially been tentative and nervous. Then the invasion had been canceled. Now he ran around just like he was at home.

Jean found the crack in the doors and tried to talk the terrified man into opening the door. The guy said he wouldn't do it because we were Voodoo Warriors. He was afraid we would eat him if he opened up. The guy was so terrified he began to talk in tongues. Jean said the guy was either an idiot or just petrified to the point of being incoherent. We decided to leave him alone.

*C-Company, 2/75 Ranger Battalion FIST in Haiti*

Over the next two days we conducted two raids on warehouses on the outskirts of town and found nothing. This whole mission, other than getting to see Haiti, was turning out to be a bust. We stayed for three days and then rotated back to GTMO ourselves. A few days later we were to re-deploy to Fort Lewis. The trip hadn't been a total loss. I had actually gotten to see a large part of the country of Haiti and although the long awaited mission never took place, the fact that every Ranger was coming home alive was a good tradeoff.

\*      \*      \*

We returned to Fort Lewis the first week of November and deployed two weeks later to the Jungle Operations Training Center (JOTC) in Panama. Again, we would work on our Jungle Operations techniques for two weeks and then redeploy home for Christmas.

We conducted the standard block of classes that we did each time we went to Panama: land navigation, poisonous snakes, waterborne operations, booby traps and counter-insurgency tactics. We would rise early and conduct physical training at dawn to avoid the heat of the day. The day would consist of the classes and then the evening was ours to relax.

LTC McChrystal had just taken command of the Battalion and this was his first chance to get a look at his men. As always, morale was high. After a week of classes, we transitioned to live fire exercises. They consisted of moving through the jungle on a predetermined azimuth and then reacting to contact with the enemy. Due to the heat and the rough terrain it was a grueling task to run these training lanes. Each platoon would do it and if the result was not to standard they would do it again. LTC McChrystal would accompany every unit through the lane to see how they functioned and he generated a lot of respect from his men. It was grueling for them to go through the lanes just one time—the boss observed each and every iteration.

The entire deployment was to culminate with a series of Company raids on various objectives that was affectionately named the "Suck Ex." That name was derived from exactly what we expected to experience. It was going to "Suck!" We made final preparations of equipment and plans in our barracks building on Camp Sherman. In two hours we would load the boats, trucks, and helicopters that would transport us to our objectives. That's when the call came to Abort Mission. I went to see the Company Commander but he was with the Colonel. I found Bob McCarthy the Company Executive Officer and asked, "What do they mean Abort Mission?" Bob said, "I don't know. We'll have to wait for the Commander to get back."

A short time later, I received the word to report to the briefing room and CPT Parks prepared to give us the scoop. Apparently Cuban refugees on the other side of the country were rioting and breaking out of their camps. We were the only unit in the country that the Southern Command could call to get the situation under control.

In the next few hours, we sent half the Battalion by helicopter and the other half by truck to the other side of the country and the outskirts of Panama City. In this area were a series of refugee camps spread along the Panama Canal. The camps were spaced with a couple miles in between and guarded only by a small military police contingent.

It was standard operating procedure for the guards to drive vehicles inside the camp to distribute supplies and conduct the administrative affairs of the camp. One day the young men in one camp had had enough and started to get violent. They hijacked a vehicle and started ramming the gate. The guards tried to block their escape but as they moved forward they were met with a shower of fist-sized rocks that shattered their plastic riot shields and inflicted numerous injuries. The Cubans got out of the wire and continued down the road.

Some headed straight for the canal and swam across to get into the suburbs of Panama City. Two bodies were found in the canal of refugees that did not swim well enough to make it across. Others drove hijacked vehicles down the road as far as they could and then fled on foot. The end result was a lot of hurt Military Police (MPs), many damaged vehicles and fugitives running wild. Also, the MPs were too beat up to try and restore order in the camps.

We moved into the wood line about two miles from the camp and waited for further instructions. If the rioters tried to come this way again, we were to stop them hand to hand. Immediately Ranger ingenuity came into play and a wide variety of clubs were quickly carved from the trees of the surrounding jungle. We remained in this position throughout the day while manning a blocking position on the road to ensure no one could pass. Our scouts moved forward to give us early warning. If the Cubans did arrive, on cue we would emerge from the jungle on their right flank, wade into them en masse and then violently subdue them. The refugees had apparently burned up their energy during the riot the day before and the afternoon passed without incident.

We waited until the evening and then moved to a hilltop overlooking the Panama Canal. There we waited again until a truck pulled up and downloaded riot gear and maul handles. The riot gear consisted of a helmet with face shield, full body Plexiglas shield and the maul handles. Since the MPs had reported that their shields had shattered under volleys of fist-sized rocks thrown by rioters, we would wear our body armor to protect the midsection of the body. We also used "100 mile an hour" tape to wrap the edges of our shields and put a big X of tape across the middle of each shield. That way if the shield shattered, from a rock hit, it would still hold together and provide some protection. "100 mile an hour" tape was much like duct tape but even stronger. Apparently it had gotten its name when Air Force ground crews left it on the outside of jets who would return from missions with the tape still attached. The Air Force also nicknamed it "mach tape."

With our equipment readied we conducted a standard rock drill of how we would assault the camp. During the night, we were to infiltrate from our position through the jungle to the wood line surrounding the compound. We would then hold our positions until 0530 hours. Then we would burst from the undergrowth and surround the camp. One platoon would cut a breach in the wire from the rear and quickly cordon off the tent housing most of the young men sleeping inside. The plan was to use maximum shock effect and surprise to overpower whoever was awake and hopefully catch most of them asleep.

With the rehearsals completed, we settled down for a last minute nap just after dark. A few minutes later a young Ranger stood up and was silhouetted against the night sky. He raised his maul handle to the sky in one hand and his shield in the other and bellowed a prayer that went something like this, "Odin, give me thy strength to carry with me into battle on the 'morrow. Let blood run upon the land as we fight for your glory. Let us rise above the shackles of tyranny and strike down the villainy of this enemy scourge!"

The whole time he was silhouetted against the moonlit sky and everything became deathly quiet as he captivated hundreds of Rangers. It sent a shiver down my spine, making me feel as if we were in a battle long ago in a far away land. It was a wild experience.

At midnight we donned our armor, formed our ranks and began marching down a road toward the camp. We hit a fork in the road where the column split. I was halfway back in the column and again it looked so damned cool. Here we were with the moonlight glistening off the top of our helmets while carrying clubs and shields as we marched in formation, like a Roman Legion, down a road and into battle. We had prepared to meet another large body of men in hand-to-hand combat; it was a scene straight from an old movie.

We moved silently in a single file through the jungle and into position outside the camps and waited for 0530. The camp was quite large, about two-hundred square meters with tents and temporary buildings spread throughout in neat rows. All was quiet except for an occasional man moving to the outhouse to relieve himself. There was a guard post fifty meters to our right with two U.S. soldiers watching the Cubans inside the fence. Other than that, no one moved.

At 0530, we burst from the jungle from the same hole in a steady stream. One after the other we flowed into the open and in seconds surrounded the camp. The breach team was in the wire instantly and the cordon established seconds later. I'll never forget what happened next. The bigger MPs jumped into the tents and started to beat the hell out of the refugees as they yelled, "Payback, Mother fuckers! How does it feel?" One by one they pulled the bleeding Cubans out and our Rangers flex cuffed them and carried them outside the wire. Once outside they laid them facedown on the grass in neat lines.

While this was happening, a Squad of female MPs came in a line right in front of us. It looked like a bunch of little girls in field hockey goalie uniforms waddling into position in front of us. They moved like the Tin Man in the Wizard of Oz. It was no wonder they had gotten their butts kicked during the refugee riot. In those suits they would have no mobility whatsoever. I could imagine what this must have looked like from the Cuban side. A bunch of little girls sitting down on the ground because they were overheating—backed by four-hundred Rangers itching for a scuffle.

*A very rare photo of Rangers restoring order to refugee camps.*

The MPs continued beating the young men until the tent was cleared out. I didn't have a good view of the men being carried out so I moved over by the guard shack for a better look. When I got close to the guards, they said, "How long were you guys sitting there in the woods?'

"Since around 0200 hours," I said back.

They shook their heads and said, "You guys scared the hell out of us. We didn't even know you were there!"

The next morning we did an identical raid on another camp where there was rumor of future unrest. There was no resistance and no beating this time. We were instructed to do a tent to tent search and we got a close look at the living conditions of these people.

We found entire families with young children doing the best they could to get by. Little rooms were made inside each tent by hanging cloth and blankets. In these rooms is where each family got their privacy. We were told to look for contraband. Contraband consisted of more than three packs of cigarettes or any large quantities of food or soap.

The entire day made me ashamed to be inside that camp. The American soldiers who were in charge of the search acted like little punks. For instance, we searched the home of a young family with two little children and one small baby. The lady had a small bread bag of bar soap that she used to clean the diapers. The idiot of a Camp Manager directed us to confiscate it because it was contraband. The whole time he said it he had a sneer on his face. I took the soap away and when the guy went to the next tent I gave it back. I felt embarrassed the whole time.

This same family had taken apart an Army cot and made two small beds for the children to sleep in. One bed could stand by itself and the other had one end tied to a post. It was a clever setup. I could imagine the relief of not having two small kids on one cot each night when the parents tried to get them to sleep. The idiot said, "Nope, this was unacceptable destruction of Government Property. It must be confiscated."

After that, the common sense rule took effect. If it made sense, we took it. If we confiscated someone's cigarettes, we left them some for goodwill. I felt sorry for these people. Some were bad apples and some were not. What a rotten place to be put for trying to get to freedom.

We completed our search and that afternoon we marched the entire formation to the refugee prison. We stood outside, looking in as a translator told the prisoners that if they acted up again we would return to kick their butts once again. That was that. We marched over the hill and loaded trucks for a little rest and recreation.

\*     \*     \*

In January, the staff, Company Commanders and Fire Support Officers headed back to the Joint Readiness Training Center (JRTC) at Fort Polk, Louisiana. This time we would execute the computer simulation side of the event as the Regimental Headquarters and 3/75 Ranger Battalion actually executed the missions in the field. The fact that we were executing a computer simulation would be transparent to the staff. We had planned as if it were the real thing. The only difference was that we would feed the information of the battle unfolding on the screens to the Tactical Operations Center who would then react as normal.

It was during this time period when the highly publicized deaths of three Ranger School candidates occurred in Florida. This was a major event that captured the headlines causing a public uproar as to how this could occur. In the Ranger community we couldn't understand what the big deal was. We had all been in those same swamps, just like those guys, and it was easy to see how it could have happened. Men die at Ranger School. It had happened in the past and usually it was due to cases of drowning in the Florida Swamp Phase.

At that same time, at JRTC, 17 Army Rangers from the 3rd Ranger Battalion were injured fast roping during an insertion. One soldier died and numerous others were hurt with everything from broken bones to sprained backs. On a pitch black night, the helicopter had kicked out the rope and the chemical lights stopped on what the Load Master and pilot thought was the ground. In reality, it was the top of 30 foot trees. As the Rangers slid down, they left the end of the rope and fell 30 feet to the ground. The Regimental Surgeon said the Ranger body armor they were wearing had actually turned out to be a blessing. It had protected their internal organs from the fall.

*Fast rope from a CH-53 PAVLO Special Operations Helicopter*

The Ranger who died came off the end of the rope and slammed into the tree. It was speculated that his helmet had gotten caught in the tree and the weight of his equipment had broken his neck or had hanged him. This was a major tragedy. A memorial was held the next day but no one questioned the event and we continued on with the mission.

Ranger School is just that—a school. The 75th Ranger Regiment is the combat unit that deploys and executes assigned missions around the world. The thing both the Regiment and the School have in common is that both are very dangerous. With the intensity of training, and all of the moving parts involved in this training, accidents are sure to happen. They will continue to happen and every man who volunteers must understand this. That is why so many do not volunteer—this is a very dangerous calling.

I left 2nd Ranger Battalion on 24 June 1995. It was a very emotional event for me. I knew my opportunities to return were very slim. Actually, because of my seven year history with the Regiment, I had an excellent chance based on personal contacts, but as the years went by the odds would stack against it. I had to get a Battery Command which could take up to four years and then forecast myself for another slot within the Regiment. That would have to time perfectly with the availability of a Ranger Battalion Fire Support Officer slot. I grew older by the day, and the toll of 230 parachute jumps was getting to my joints.

It wasn't a matter of staying in shape. In many ways, I was in the best shape of my life. I could still run two miles in 12 minutes and 30 seconds, do 100 pushups and 90 sit-ups in two minutes each and do 15 pull-ups. The problem was my right ankle and back. My right interior ankle bone had a huge bump on it from a bone chip. The same ankle had a degenerating joint. Together, the bump and joint gave me constant pain. My lower right back also constantly ached from that same nasty jump during a runway clearing operation.

We were conducting a parachute jump onto an airfield and about one-hundred feet from the ground an Air Force Combat Control Team member passed underneath me. He stole the air from my parachute and I felt myself go into a free fall toward the ground. I just maintained the best body position I could to lessen the impact and landed on the concrete shoulder of the runway. I hit so hard that my metal canteen cup was flattened and the canteen of water inside it exploded under the impact of my body.

I laid there not daring to move and feeling extreme pain throughout my body. *I'm fucked up. I'm fucked up,* I thought to myself as I tried to clear my head. After a couple of minutes, I started moving my limbs to assess my situation. All the parts moved and the pain subsided. I gingerly packed my gear and gimped the hundred yards to my assembly area. The pain was excruciating but the only damage turned out to be a cracked ankle and bruised right side. I wouldn't have it evaluated by a doctor for two more weeks. By that time it was too late in the healing process to remove the chip.

It was time to make a decision on which route to take with my career. I could continue with a conventional artillery career and make a decision to return to the Regiment or take a Joint service assignment later as a Fire Support planner. I could also make the long over due shift over to Special Forces and work on an "A" Team. My childhood buddy, Randy Earp, had been after me for years to come over to the "other side." My biggest reservation with the Green Berets was they were not a direct action unit. Yes, they had special teams tailored for covert operations, but their major mission was to train indigenous people to fight for themselves.

I still wanted to be where the action was and that would be with a maneuver unit. It didn't matter if it was with a mechanized or light unit—it just had to be in the thick of things. I decided to stick with the Field Artillery.

# Chapter 7
## Cold Winds

I began dealing with my placement Officer at the Department of the Army and was offered the option to go to Hawaii. I said, "There's no way I'd ever get an assignment that good!" I thought he was joking. He wasn't and I was headed to Hawaii ... after a year in Korea.

I whined for weeks to my branch manager MAJ Ken Boehm but it didn't matter; I had to go to Korea. They had to fill a quota and I hadn't been stationed overseas in ten years of service. It was still considered a hot spot in the world considering a treaty had never been signed in the 1950's. The countries had signed an armistice and faced each other over the most fortified border in the world for forty years.

Korea was a particularly unstable situation during the past two years because of the death of their Prime Minister, threats to develop nuclear weapons, and threats to invade the South. Because their economy was so diminished, it was thought the North Koreans might actually invade in the near future in an act of desperation. If the government was so unstable, combined with famine from a failed rice crop, an invasion attempt or international incident could divert the attention of the North Koreans from their economic and famine problems.

On 3 January 1996, I flew out of Los Angeles International Airport. We flew a military charter jet to Anchorage, Alaska then onto Seoul, South Korea. Three-thousand miles and twenty hours later I got my first look at Korea. My first impression was it looked like West Virginia or Pennsylvania. Maybe even the rolling hill country around the Mississippi and Missouri rivers throughout the Midwest with open farmland surrounded by large, hardwood covered hills. It was overcast, rainy, and snow was on the ground.

We got off the plane, loaded onto buses and drove to downtown Seoul to a four star hotel called the Dragon Hill Lodge. Since we had arrived on a Friday we got to stay there at government expense for the weekend. What a deal! The next few days were spent walking around the hotel grounds, meeting other people coming into the country and trying to get used to seeing so many oriental people.

The following Monday I received my orders and rode a bus to Camp Casey located about two hours north of Seoul. In bus time, that meant we were about fifty miles from the capital on very congested little roads. We immediately moved into the Personnel Processing Center referred to as the "Turtle Farm." It consisted of old Quonset huts whose round shaped roofs resembled the shell of a turtle. For two days, we filled out paperwork, received briefings on the Korean situation, and an orientation to the area. On the third day a vehicle arrived to transport three of us to the 1-15 Field Artillery, a 155mm self-propelled howitzer unit which directly supported the 1st Brigade, 2nd Infantry Division (Mechanized).

The 1-15 FA at Camp Casey sat only fifteen files from the Demilitarized Zone (DMZ) established along the 38th parallel after the Armistice ended the war. Being fifteen miles from enemy artillery is an unsettling thought. That meant that if hostilities broke out we were within a lanyard pull, plus time of flight, from the enemy artillery and the North Koreans had a lot of artillery. In fact, they outnumbered us in artillery pieces fifteen to one.

As soon as I walked into the compound, familiar faces began to pop up from all directions. Numerous Officers and NCOs were there from my days in the 4th ID in Fort Carson. Everywhere I went I ran into somebody I knew. At the equipment issue facility a NCO stopped me and said, "Hey Sir, do you remember me?"

"No, I don't think so." I replied.

"I taught demolitions and booby traps at the Jungle Operations Training Center in Panama. You came through my lane," he said with a big smile on his face.

I shook his hand vigorously and said, "Damn, this is a small world."

*MAJ Hansen, CPT Dave Grimes and me in the 1-15 FA TOC*

The new officers soon had an audience with the Battalion Commander. We filed into the office of LTC Eduardo Cardenas and he broke the news as to what our jobs would be for the next year. I would be the Assistant S-3 for operations. That meant that I would manage the land, ammunition, firing points and training assets of the Battalion. In wartime, I would manage the Tactical Operations Center (TOC) ensuring the planning and execution of the Field Artillery Support Plan. Of course, I was the assistant to the S-3 so it was my job to make sure nothing fell through the cracks.

I arrived just in time to head with the Battalion to the field for out first big training event "WARSTEED '96". This was my first indoctrination into the Korean cold. The terrain and conditions initially reminded me of Fort Carson, Colorado—a lot of snow in the valleys surrounded by small mountains. The nights were very cold and I stayed up throughout each night conducting training and ensuring our plans were completed on time.

The TOC consisted of tent extensions off the back of four M577 personnel carrier (armored tracks) and zipped together into one big room. This space was heated by two Yukon stoves fueled by kerosene and MOGAS (a mixture of diesel fuel and gasoline). Kerosene burned cooler than MOGAS but also reduced the fire risk. On a frosty night these two Yukon stoves could barely take the chill out of the air. On a cold night it was miserable inside the TOC. I actually would spend some late hours straddling the stoves and letting it bake me in an attempt to warm up. It was ridiculously cold and we tried to stay warm any way we could.

We returned from the field and started the next years training cycle. Each year was the same—new people, a new training cycle, and it culminated at the next year's WARSTEED. The hours were long and tedious but because I had so much work to do, time flew by. For two months, I worked seven days each week on projects that I felt needed to be accomplished to get the office up to speed. During this period, I didn't have much help from the staff and a re-organization was quickly executed. I distributed the workload of the shop and at the end of the third month we finally broke out of the end of the work tunnel.

About that time the Operations Officer, MAJ Camp, left for the Pentagon and a new job. His replacement would not arrive for two more months. I assumed his duties as the interim S-3 and, lucky for me, a new operations NCO named SFC Victor Putnam arrived in the Battalion. He was very experienced, professional, and aggressive. We developed an instant rapport.

Together we made improvements within the shop and projected training and resources into the next year. No piece of information came in or went out of the office without both of us seeing it. Nothing in writing was released out of the shop without my proofing it first. Anything that left our office would reflect how we operated and we wanted there to be no doubt we were a very professional and efficient operation. The shop hummed with efficiency, the staff was comfortable with their responsibilities, and for two months I ran the 1-15 Field Artillery.

I don't say that in jest; everyone knew it. The old Battalion commander was intent on leaving and the new commander LTC Mike Fitzgerald would not arrive for another month. He would then have to get his feet on the ground to see what was going on. The S-3 and Battalion Sergeant Major were already gone so the only Command Group member left was the Battalion Executive Officer (XO). He was busy with the maintenance nightmares of the Battalion, and I had a free hand to schedule, resource and drive the training focus of the Battalion. I would stop and see the XO for my daily sanity check while making sure he was up to date on what I was doing. He had a way of looking at events from a completely different angle than me. Combine that with the wealth of his experience, add in the contrasting views I maintained, and it gave me a warm and fuzzy feeling that the Battalion was moving in the right direction, as we awaited our new commander.

On 5 April 1996, the situation along the DMZ became increasingly tense. North Korea announced that they would no longer abide by the Armistice that had governed the conduct of forces along the DMZ since the 1950's. Two days prior, a senior North Korean official announced to the Soviet Union that the state of affairs between North and South Korea and the United States had become intolerable. He told the Soviet parliament that it wasn't a matter of "if" but of "when" war would begin again.

I went to the Emergency Operations Center (EOC) to see if any communications from the 2nd Infantry Division had come in during the day. The Staff Duty Officer said that DivArty had directed that all Battalion Commanders and higher must be reachable within fifteen minutes. That indicated the Korean theater did respect the threat developing along the DMZ although it wasn't great enough to alert any units. The Korean command had flexibility built into the system because U.S. forces continuously maintained an increased readiness posture. If we alerted troops and rolled to the field, the North would immediately be notified by their spies in the area. Any move of that magnitude would be considered provocative. The United States would not want to trigger a major event.

On 6 April, North Korea moved Company sized infantry units into the DMZ armed with heavy machine guns. This was considered a significant development because it exceeded the allowable forces prescribed by the Armistice. The North had done what it had promised and disregarded the rules that had held the Armistice together for forty years.

The Republic of (South) Korea (ROK) units along the border responded by increasing their patrolling and reconnaissance efforts but basically remained in a wait and see posture. The United Nations Command was trying to downplay the incident and planned to make a formal complaint to the United Nations governing council. They felt that North Korea had made provocative moves in the past and this most likely would just blow over.

Around three o'clock in the afternoon, I went to the Emergency Operations Center to check the messages. Two messages had come in from DivArty; neither was classified. They talked about the current situation and the need for Operational Security (OPSEC). During the next few days, the Soviet Union and China put pressure on North Korea to maintain the Armistice along the Demilitarized Zone (DMZ). After three days of illegal incursions, the forays into the neutral zone stopped. The question was what were they trying to accomplish?

On 11 April, I went to a meeting with the Battalion Commander to brief the brigades Quarterly Training Status to Major General (MG) Tommy Franks, the Division Commander. After the conclusion of the briefing, MG Franks addressed his Battalion commanders. "Gentleman, we don't know what the North Koreans are trying to accomplish along the DMZ. Some of you may think you know, but in reality you don't. No one does. This is a people we just don't understand. Commanders look at me! Stop writing and look at me and hear what I am telling you. I want you to be aware of your surroundings. I want you to be safe. You are important men. Do you realize how valuable you are to this Brigade and this Division? I want you to be careful because I would feel damn bad if you were assassinated or kidnapped, probably the former, and we can't afford to lose you. So until this situation along the DMZ calms down you all take extra care of yourselves. Any questions?"

The entire issue of action along the DMZ took a wait and see posture. On 17 April President Clinton visited South Korea during his Asian Tour. He held a news conference with the

South Korean President on Cheju Island and announced a plan for joint peace talks.

The North Korean goal had always been a peace treaty with the United States while ignoring the existence of South Korea. The U.S. had always rejected any such talks and said that any peace talks had to be between North and South Korea. What made this proposal unique was it called for both Koreas, the U.S., and China to have joint peace talks as soon as possible. China and the U.S. had been the primary backers of both sides during the Korean conflict. It was felt that this forum might entice North Korea to sit down at the table once and for all.

Things remained tense along the border for the next few weeks with the north continuing to send small groups of soldiers into the DMZ. In late May, the soldiers moved into the DMZ and fired their weapons into the air. They left after the South fired warning shots over their heads.

On 25 May, a North Korean pilot defected to the South by flying his MIG fighter jet across the DMZ. He was met by two American F-16s and escorted to a secure runway. He said he couldn't live with the system in the north and left a wife and two kids behind. The family left behind is usually sentenced to hard labor camps to set an example for anyone else who might be thinking about it. Also, five North Korean Navy vessels steamed across the informal border off the coast of the Korean peninsula. They returned immediately pursued by South Korean ships.

While on my mid-tour leave back to Iowa I decided I just couldn't stay in Korea and called the Officer Assignment Branch to request an assignment to Fort Campbell and the 101st Air Assault Division. The next day the telephone rang and it was a call from Korea. I was offered the opportunity to command the HHB 1-15 Field Artillery at Camp Casey. I had the choice of getting an immediate command in a far away place or getting back to the states with the opportunity of having a series of assignments in a good unit.

Two factors hit me and made my decision easy. If I were going to be a thousand miles away from my family anyway, why not be four-thousand miles away. The other factor was the desire to get back to Special Operations. The fever was starting to burn in my stomach and this command was my passport back to the 'dark side.' The next day I accepted the command and departed for Korea one week early.

Soon after I returned to South Korea, a North Korean submarine was found run aground off the coast, one-hundred miles east of Seoul. Eight dead bodies were found on the beach and the locals had seen numerous men heading into the wood line. The ROK army mobilized forty-thousand troops to look for the infiltrators and the hunt was on. In the first couple days, a North Korean commando was captured and revealed that the submarine had run aground while dropping off commandos who intended to complete an unknown mission. He related that when the sub got stuck, the Commandos killed the crew and then moved inland. The total number of infiltrators totaled twenty-nine. Over the next few weeks numerous firefights and ambushes accounted for twenty-six of the commandos. All were killed except for the man in custody. The North denied any knowledge of any infiltrators, but did want their submarine back. A month later, three commandos remained unaccounted for.

\*        \*        \*

On 30 September 1996, I took command of Headquarters and Headquarters Battery, 1-15 Field Artillery, Camp Casey, Korea. I told the men standing in formation that it was a "wild" moment for me to be taking command of a battery eleven years after I had enlisted in the Army as a Private First Class. I promised we would work hard, play hard, and have a lot of fun over the next year.

Two days later, I spoke to the enlisted soldiers to let them know about myself, my command philosophy and to hear any comments or concerns. The soldiers had the typical complaints about chow, room space and physical training being too easy. The Korean Augmentees to the United States Army (KATUSA) soldiers wanted better relations with their American counterparts and some added responsibility. The soldiers seemed to take a lot of pleasure in the fact that I had been an enlisted soldier and listened intently as I talked.

In my philosophy, I told them I was a very simple and common sense professional soldier. I believed in emphasizing what was important, that every soldier be ready to engage and kill any enemy that we might face. I believed in the major killing systems in the arms room which were to have our people trained and ready to send steel down range and defeat the North Koreans whenever they decided they were going to come. They were going to come ... their entire national goal was to take the South and unify the peninsula. They made no bones about it. Sooner or later they were going to come and we had to be ready.

I told them only forty years ago their grandfathers and my uncles had fought and died here. We were here to ensure that the communists never take this country. The President, Congress, and the American people determined we were going to defend this piece of ground. That's exactly what we would do or die in place taking as many of the enemy with us as we could. I later told the NCOs the same thing. Plus, if they couldn't look themselves in the mirror on Friday night thinking my men are trained, my equipment is ready and my vehicle is ready to roll, then they were failing their mission. We were only thirty seconds away from enemy artillery. Therefore, it was very likely we would have to fight from the motor pool or from positions around Camp Casey.

I would not play any peacetime training crap. We would train the way we planned to fight. We would take all crew served with weapons, ice packs, night vision and communications equipment every time we went to the field. I also assured them that I would immediately move enough ammunition to the arms room. Then when we moved to the field we could protect ourselves until the first log pack arrived. They looked at me with mouths and eyes wide open.

I had no plans to make a lot of immediate changes in the battery until I had a chance to assess each area. A few things did need immediate attention. One-third of my night vision goggles were inoperable. My Crew Served Weapons (heavy machine guns) were not properly assigned and it was obvious the soldiers didn't know how to care for or operate this essential equipment. Especially the Korean Augmentees to the United States Army (KATUSAs), who thought night vision goggles were like glasses and had an individual prescription. They would look into the totally blurry goggles and think, *These things are not my prescription and therefore worthless.* They didn't even know how to focus them! I put a KATUSA on a guard post and asked him if he knew how to use the dummy claymore mine at the position. He didn't even know what it was. We had a serious problem!

My second week in command we deployed to the field for four days to execute an artillery live fire exercise. After we returned, the next week was for recovery of equipment from the field. I inspected the arms room finding weapons and night vision goggles still unclean. To make matters worse, we were up to twenty-five sets of unserviceable PVS-7 Night Vision Goggles. This was totally unacceptable and against my entire command emphasis. As luck would have it I happened to run into Colonel Harris the Commander of our support units. "Sir, I've been in command for twenty-four days and for twenty-four days, I have been trying to turn in eighteen sets of NVGs to the 302 Forward Support Battalion. They won't take them." His eyes got narrow and he said, "I'll take care of it." Ten minutes later he sent me a message saying it was fixed. That Friday was to be a Battalion training holiday but the battery was in such a state of disrepair that I decided to work instead. I could return the holiday to the battery at a later date—after our readiness had improved.

Friday morning at 0800 we had a battery formation. After the promotion of two soldiers I had the battery fall in around me. "Okay, this is why we're here this morning. I inspected the arms room. The weapons and night vision goggles are dirty. I told the NCOs when I got here that if you can't look yourself in the mirror on Friday night and know that your men are trained, your equipment ready, and your vehicle ready to roll then you are failing your mission. I would be a damned hypocrite to allow us to go on a three-day weekend when I know, for a fact, that we are not trained and our equipment is not ready. This week General Timmons, the 8th Army Commander, and General Franks, the 2nd ID Commander, both said you can look at a units arms room and if their weapons and night vision are clean, their vehicles ready and their soldiers trained to use that equipment that is all you need to look at to see what kind of unit you have got. I must be pretty smart or we must all think alike. I had Senior NCOs come up to me and say I need to go somewhere else to command like the 82nd or the 101st. You know something men? The 82nd and 101st are a long way from the enemy. We are in the right place! Thirty miles to the west and twenty-five miles to the north is the 4th largest army in the world. Sixty-percent of it is sitting on the border. In the first minute, there will be 239,000 artillery rounds coming south. That doesn't count the contrails from the FROG medium range missiles flying all the way to Pusan (as I pointed at the sky). This is where the enemy is and we need to be ready. We can range all of our targets right from here on Camp Casey. We need to have our bags packed so when we hear the rolling thunder of artillery in the distance we can grab our gear and equipment and disperse around Camp Casey. Men, that is why we are here. This morning we are going to refresh ourselves on the claymore mine, M-203 grenade launcher, the SAW (Squad Automatic Machine gun) and our night vision. If you have questions, ask! Then we will clean the weapons again, and when we are done, we can all have a weekend knowing we are ready to fight and win if we need to."

The soldiers were fired up. Some of the NCOs and my XO came in and said it was "WHOO-AH!" It set the tone for the training and as I rotated from class to class the soldiers were intently paying attention and participating. Everyone had to have hands on and do each event themselves. It was a good day.

At the beginning of my second month, major problems surfaced and forced me to make decisions that could jeopardize my authority as Battery Commander. I commanded a Battery of over 257 soldiers and over 50 vehicles, which is the equivalent of a small Battalion. These soldiers, vehicles and their associated equipment were spread over five Battalions, in two

Brigades, on three different posts. It was an accountability nightmare.

I had grand ideas but failed to recognize that every program in existence in Korea had come from years of experience from men that were long gone. Veterans of Korea said the U.S. military had been in Korea for forty years, one year at a time, because of the annual personnel turn over. The problems started when new leaders arrived from the states and thought the systems or procedures they brought with them were better than those already in use. A new system would then be emplaced and slowly over the year, the system changed until it went full circle back to the original.

I had consolidated all but one Task Force of weapons in my arms room when we realized during an alert we could not issue the weapons fast enough to the FIST, the Guard Force, and the Battery to meet the alert timeline. We improved our arms room issue procedures, doubled the manpower, operated two issue windows and still couldn't meet the times. I then made the decision to move one Task Force of weapons back to maneuver arms rooms and not bring in the other. It was a common sense idea that did not work and I'm sure someone else had figured that out a long time ago.

My focus and expectations as a Commander were beginning to change. I had thought that the war fighting capability of my unit would be the measure of success. The definition of a successful command now could be summed as keeping accountability of your equipment, keeping your men out of trouble, having zero cold weather injuries, keeping your maintenance program up to reportable standards, and keeping your reportable statistics up to the 90% standard.

Each month Battalion Commanders would have to send Unit Status Reports to the Department of the Army. These were statuses on weapons qualifications, physical readiness, overweight programs, legal actions, dental and medical readiness and much more. If a unit reported under the 90% standard they come under immediate scrutiny from above. Questions then snowballed from the highest levels for a justification. It went all the way up and all the way down the chain of command. This pressure to achieve those statistics created an environment where the urge to pad the numbers was tremendous. No one wanted to be the one not making the standard. The result was questionable numbers.

It also forced units to take time away from real readiness to work the statistics. For example, every soldier was expected to zero his personal weapon within the first thirty days in country. This would allow him, in an emergency, to shoot and kill an enemy with his weapon. The problem was there was a shortage of rounds regularly available in Korea for training. If a Commander needed to reallocate a new soldier's zero rounds to get his Battery's qualification stats up to 90% and not get his butt chewed, it forced him into a small ethical decision. If no rounds at all were available, the padding of numbers became common. The month before I took command, the Battery statistics were all in the 90% range. After I took command, I told my training room we would not lie about any reported statistic. There had to be records to prove it. The result was my statistics dropped into the 30% range.

The combat readiness of our unit was the number one most important area of emphasis for me. I guess because of my Special Operations background being ready on a no notice basis was essential. Many decisions began to be made in the Battalion regarding our readiness that made absolutely no sense to this old Ranger and totally unsettled me.

It was decided by the Battalion Commander and Executive Officer that we would download the ammunition out of our Field Artillery Ammunition Support Vehicles (FAASV) into the

Ammunition Holding Area (AHA) about a mile up the road. This ammunition had always been maintained in these vehicles so in time of war we could just upload the rounds into the howitzers and either shoot from Camp Casey or get off post to avoid enemy incoming artillery fires.

The first mention of this came in a Battalion training meeting and I almost spilled my coffee on myself as I heard it discussed. I immediately joined the discussion and made it clear I thought it was a bad idea due to the North Korean threat and the real possibility that war could come at any moment on this peninsula. I said it was a known fact that our AHAs were targeted by both enemy artillery and SOF forces. To think we would have time to get to the AHA and load that ammunition was accepting a lot of risk. If we deployed downrange for a training exercise and the "balloon went up," we would have to fight our way back to post through civilian traffic to get our ammunition before we could fight. By having it with us, we could fight on a moments notice.

My position seemed to have some effect but in the end the decision was made to download the ammunition to ease accountability problems and wear and tear on the vehicles. The Commander decided to accept the risk and it did not make me happy. Maybe I was just too much of an extremist or readiness purist. Wasn't this Korea? Weren't we the defenders of Freedom's Frontier? Wasn't the Red Hoard only twenty miles away? The Tank and Infantry Battalions seemed to think so. They still kept their ammunition uploaded and with them wherever they went.

After the meeting I stopped the Battalion XO on the step and wanted to make clear my concerns. I told him I wouldn't be a Commander unless I made it perfectly clear how strong I felt on this topic. I let him know that I felt we were making a terrible mistake and we wouldn't know just how big a mistake until the

North Koreans decided to come south. He explained that for maintenance and accountability it made good sense. The best estimate said we would have at least ten days warning of imminent hostilities. I countered that we didn't give the North Koreans enough credit to figure out they could fix us in place with their 15 to 1 artillery advantage long enough to move their maneuver forces to the border. If the AHA was targeted, there would likely be no ammunition left to draw.

The conversation was pointless but at least I had said my piece. Regardless, the decision had been made and I had to answer the same questions from my men that I had just asked. It raised a major question as to just how important any talk of readiness was to this whole mission.

December came and with it the annual St. Barbara's Day Ball. St. Barbara is the patron saint of the Artillery and "The Order of St Barbara" had been established to honor artillery men who had made an impact and distinguished themselves in the artillery community. Usually senior NCOs and Officers in the grade of Captain and above were inducted. There were, of course, a few exceptions to include civilians and high ranking personnel from other branches. I would be inducted at this ceremony along with around forty other soldiers. Regardless of who was inducted it was a good excuse for a big party and this was to be no exception.

The ceremony would include the history of St. Barbara. She was the daughter of a King in the fourth century and was kept prisoner in a tower to protect her from the outside world. The entire kingdom including her father was pagan. St. Barbara somehow found out about Christianity and took up the faith. She had only one window in the tower to view the outside world. Apparently during a storm lightening struck the tower forming a second window. While her father was away at war, she had a third window placed in the room, thus representing the holy Trinity and representative of Christianity.

When her father returned from war and found out about the windows, he was so angered he beheaded his daughter himself. As he rode from the field of the execution he was struck by lightening and killed. St. Barbara became the patron saint of lightening and then artillery because of the clap of thunder and flash of lightening it delivers.

After the ball ended, I was walking across the parking lot on my way to the post party at the Officer's Club and bumped into Brigadier General Jackson on the way to his vehicle. BG Jackson had been the Ranger Regimental Commander during operations in Haiti. The last time I had seen him had been on the *USS America* and he seemed genuinely pleased to see me. He asked how I was doing and I told him I was in command. He asked what I would do after command and I said I was thinking about returning to the Regiment one more time as a Battalion Fire Support Officer. He stopped walking, looked at me and said I had better think carefully about that idea. He said my Branch didn't look too favorably on that, and I should consider other options. I said I understood, but I had a burning desire to get back to Special Ops if I could. He said to give it some thought and if it was what I really wanted to do I should go ahead and do it. It threw me off my game a bit to have a past Regimental Commander telling me not to go back to the Regiment!

Life in Korea was very different than in the United States for service members during their off duty hours. The soldiers were four-thousand miles from home and they were very lonely to say the least. The Koreanswere very resourceful people and they, of course, had tapped into this American weakness by providing an entertainment district outside of every American base. At Camp Casey it was called the "Ville." Tong Du Chon

(TDC) is a small town of around twenty-thousand people with an American sector of shops and clubs.

Inside this sector were retail shops where you could buy counterfeit clothes, purses, shoes, jewelry, watches and sports apparel that you may desire. The nighttime entertainment consisted of an assortment of clubs and bars tailored to attract the young American soldier. Strip clubs, prostitutes, dance clubs, and drinking bars made up the five-block area.

When you combined that environment with the fact that military men worked hard, trained hard and spent long periods of time in the field, those small windows of social opportunity were a prime time for trouble. Statistics said there was a 400% increase in incidents in 1996 compared to the previous four years. I personally believe this was a result of a 400% increase in the number of Military Police and Courtesy Patrols looking for any incident combined with a no tolerance attitude.

In the past if you had a scuffle, you would call the soldier's chain of command. If a soldier was drunk, you would take him home. If a drunken soldier was taking a pee in the bushes, you would chew him out and send him on his way or call his supervisor. Not anymore. Every little violation was an incident and the violator hauled into the police station. His name would come down on a blotter report (daily roll up of arrests) that arrived on the Division Commander's desk each day. The whole thing was ridiculous! Don't get me wrong. Serious incidents needed to be treated as such and the offender punished but this *no tolerance* environment was ruining a lot of good young men's careers.

In my fourth month of command, it was time for me to contact the Department of the Army and try to get a good follow-on assignment for after I left Korea. I would be a Command Qualified Captain and that offered different assignment opportunities than Captains still waiting for command. I, on the other hand, would leave Korea with that hurdle completed and a whole different set of opportunities were supposedly available. They usually fell into a few areas. Reserves, Recruiting, ROTC, Joint Assignments, Functional Areas, or Master Degree Programs accounted for most slots.

I had completed tough assignments for my entire first twelve years of service and it was time for me to get something to benefit me. That, of course, meant a slot within the Ranger Regiment, Special Operations Command, Joint Special Operations Command, or a Joint Service job. I felt I had paid my dues and it was time for something lucrative to come my way. My backup plan was already in place and that involved the long overdue shift to Special Forces and the Green Berets. It wasn't what I really wanted, but it was my safety valve.

*       *       *

On 26 January 1997, I received a telephone call at 6 a.m. *"Is this Captain Combs? Captain Combs of Staff Sergeant Combs of 3rd Ranger Battalion fame? The same Staff Sergeant Combs that got kicked out of Shoney's for fighting?"*

I answered carefully into the phone, *"Yes?"*

*"This is Sergeant Bruce Avramis at the DivArty TOC."*

I exclaimed, *"How's it going, Bruce?"*

Bruce had been with me at the Shoney's Breakfast Bar brawl and was the guy who had pulled my truck up to the door and drove me to the hospital. We had just said hello and then he gave me a Red Cross message for one of my soldiers. That was Army life; acquaintances popped in and out of the picture.

The entire training period of October '96 through January '97 was spent in preparation for the annual major External Evaluation of the year in the Korean theater—WARSTEED, Korea's equivalent of NTC. A full evaluation team would marry down on our Battalion. They would closely watch our ability to alert, transition to war, shoot, move, and communicate in a tactical environment. Countless hours had been spent reviewing and practicing Standard Operating Procedure. We were ready to ensure we could execute our missions to the highest standard.

At 0500 hours, on 12 of February 1997, 1-15 Field Artillery received the alert notification for WARSTEED '97. In less than ten minutes, the entire Battalion was a beehive of activity as it executed its mission to alert, upload, and depart Camp Casey in the shortest time possible. Four hours later the mission was completed and the Battalion stood ready to depart the camp when ordered.

There was no doubt that the countless rehearsals and preparations had paid great dividends. In the first After Action Review (AAR) that covered this event, there was nothing but the highest praise for all areas of the transition to war. The Battalion then deployed to the field and for five days and fired its howitzers against time and accuracy standards to evaluate its ability to complete the mission.

My Battery supported the operations of the gun batteries by providing communications, logistics, and administrative and tactical control. This all came from the Combat Trains where I was located. My unit consisted of thirty-seven vehicles, which occupied a three-hundred meter square piece of terrain and established a secure perimeter. The Combat Trains had elements from the medics, survey, communications, NBC, maintenance, fuel trucks, ammunition carriers and the Tactical Operations Center (TOC) itself.

Once we occupied a position, security was established, the TOC became operational and perimeter improvement began. We had occupied an open field with a small berm along the south side. The First Sergeant and I designated five crew served weapon positions to be turned into sandbagged bunkers with machine guns defending in a 360 degree perimeter.

The positions had been occupied but the men said the ground was too hard to dig holes for the fighting positions. I said, "That's crap and I'll prove it!" I grabbed a pick and moved to a position and started swinging. Forty minutes later I had gotten down two inches on a three-foot square area and had a change of heart. "OK, if we can't dig down, get the bags and we'll build up." A day later we had five hardened positions with range cards and communications. What we lacked was overhead cover to protect against enemy artillery. I took a KATUSA into the nearby village, borrowed five pieces of plywood from the locals and by the afternoon we had a layer of sandbags over our heads.

Outside the pickets were three strands of concertina wire and pickets which would slow advancing infantry. All posts and sections inside the perimeter were wired to a telephone hot loop ending at the First Sergeant's and my vehicles—this was the "Helldawg" Command Post.

On the third day, the enemy infantry attacked our perimeter. They had tried to attack us at our weakest moment, which was during the dinner meal. They had hoped to catch us with our guard down during chow time. An hour earlier we had seen a suspicious vehicle moving around the area. PFC Joshua Smith, my driver, and I made a 360-degree security sweep with our vehicle. We were just completing the sweep when we stopped to look along a railroad track 200 yards from our wire. As PFC Smith relieved himself on the tracks he said, "Hey sir, grab the binoculars. There's somebody down the tracks a ways!" I grabbed the binoculars, and sure enough, the OPFOR was trying to sneak up on us. They saw us identify them and ran for the wire. If they could, they would get close enough to throw an explosive charge into the TOC and take it out.

I quickly called on the radio, alerted my Lieutenant and he alerted the Combat Trains. In seconds, the men were in defensive positions along the wire and waiting for the OPFOR. Meanwhile, my driver and I moved to the berm and "killed" each OPFOR as he left the grass and ran for the wire. The Observer Controller saw what was happening and yelled at us on the berm saying, "You're dead! Lay down and stop shooting!"

The Battery occupied a position located on the top of a bluff overlooking a river a one-hundred feet below. We were to occupy this position providing command and control as the artillery fired in support of the Brigade as it attacked to the east.

We had the Division Artillery Fire Finding Radar attached to the Combat Trains. I had the engineers dig it into a survivability position in the middle of the perimeter.

This radar was used to detect enemy artillery firing on friendly forces and then send the location to our artillery which would fire a response. Our radar was considered a High Payoff Target to the opposition and a critical node to the friendly forces. My guidance for COL Hartsell, the DivArty Commander, was crystal clear, "If you lose that radar I will cut your nuts off." I had no intention of losing that radar. My men strung 1,100 meters of triple strand concertina wire around three sides of the perimeter. The fourth side was our back which was butted up against the bluff. The Battalion TOC and the Radar were both bermed in and surrounded again by triple strand concertina.

The defense was four-tiered. First, we had counter-reconnaissance and ambush patrols. Second, we had Listening Posts/Observation Posts (LP/OPs) outside the perimeter. This consisted of two men watching and listening for any approaching enemy. Third, we had Squad-sized fighting positions and crew served weapons inside circular berms with interlocking fields of fire. Last, we had bermed positions for the TOC and Radar. These positions were separately defended from within with long open fields of fire. To get into the perimeter would be difficult. To get within hand grenade distance of the targets would be very difficult.

To augment the defense, we deployed over fifty trip flares on all avenues of approach to the hill top. The First Sergeant and I had decided that if we had an "Achilles Heel" it would be a determined Light Infantry climbing up the bluff to our rear. It was then decided that we would climb halfway down the bluff to a long wooded ledge and "wire" it with flares to ensure the enemy did not climb up and hide in position until ready to strike.

The First Sergeant took great pride in his trip flare skills and soon was putting the first flare into place. After he had it up he began to camouflage it with leave and brush. As he was putting the last leaf on I thought to myself, "He's going to set it off." A split second later, "WHOOSH!" and the sparks rained down on the leaves below and a brushfire started. The First Sergeant attempted to stomp it out while sitting on his butt. I pulled him away by the underarms. The fire spread quickly. Twenty soldiers on the side of the bluff could not put it out. Every time we would put out what we could reach, it would flare up from below the cliff and start again.

Another Battery was in position around the bend of the river. They said it looked like a billboard of fire as the whole bluff burned. Later that evening fire trucks were called in and the flame extinguished. I had to use sign language to explain to the Fire Marshall how the bluff caught on fire. He seemed satisfied and left the scene. I wasn't the one who had set the flare off but as the story spread it was distorted to the effect that "the Ranger" did it. The DivArty Commander just looked at me, rolled his eyes and laughed. I guess he was just happy that radar was still safe.

In the end, the Battery exceeded all expectations. They received a "Trained" status in all areas of evaluation. The evaluators couldn't understand why the men were so extremely motivated. The men had done a great job and it was all to their credit. The remainder of my tour in Command, and for that matter Korea, seemed anti-climactic after such a motivating training event. It was a standard tour of duty for a Battery Commander—supply accountability, maintenance, training and caring for my soldiers. It was long, tedious and stressful work but I knew it was potentially the only command I would have in my career and I wanted to do it right.

In the early spring, I started to make some weekend forays down to Seoul to see what was there. The trip consisted of taking a two-hour American bus ride through the hectic Korean traffic or a one hour subway ride fighting the populace for some space and maybe just a seat. It was very common to have an old lady nudge and push past you and grab a seat. If you were in a seat and stood up to offer it to an old lady, a young Korean would jump into it and leave the old lady standing there. It was very frustrating and you had to forget about being polite and having a bubble of space about you.

Seoul offered a completely different environment than TDC did to the north. It had a large population of Caucasian foreigners in the country to teach, attend college, business opportunities, tourists or to just be a bum. All of the people hung out around the Yongsan Army Base and the surrounding area giving a different feel to the city. Modern buildings, traffic, businesses and slightly more polite people catered to this different worldly crowd.

In September of 1997, I joined a guided tour of the Demilitarized Zone and the Conference Table where the Armistice had been signed. It was a very interesting tour of the DMZ, its defenses, and the tunnels that the North had attempted to dig under the DMZ in order to infiltrate large numbers of infantry and attack the defenses from the south.

While in the conference hall, the North Korean guards stood a few feet away at the windows watching us inside the building. They seemed to be gaunt and stoic soldiers in what I considered bland dress uniforms. It was interesting to view firsthand this enemy which had proven his determination in battle a generation before—unimposing but always potentially dangerous.

We left the DMZ and headed south to Camp Casey. The tour wasn't an eye-opening event but definitely of value to the younger soldiers. Many were impressed and had their close proximity to possible hostilities brought to their attention.

\*    \*    \*

It was during this time that I experienced a situation so very common in military life. My first wife and I divorced. The commonality of this in the service is far wider than many would expect. The recipe is set for disaster. Years of deployment and separation along with the uncertainty for what lay ahead. In Special Operations, if you weren't on your second or third marriage you were an anomaly; I wasn't an anomaly. The joke was that a soldier would DX (Direct Exchange) his wife. This meant to turn her in to the Central Issue Facility (CIF) like a piece of broken equipment and await the reissue of a new replacement.

The decision for divorce was basically made halfway into my Korea tour for me—at the beginning of my tour for my wife at the time. The issue festered but it had to wait until I returned to be completed. During the interim is when I had the great fortune to meet my new girlfriend who would meet me in the U.S. and become my next partner in life. She was Kiwi girl who had been teaching English in Seoul to Korean kids with an appetite to learn the English language. Interestingly, when we met people in Iowa they would ask where she was from. When she replied in her English accent, "New Zealand." The next question would be, "Really … what language do they speak there?"

*1SGWilliams in Korea looking after me.*

# Chapter 8
## Change of Mission

Timing was everything and for me meant a tour as an Army Reserve Officers' Training Corps (ROTC) instructor to await a better opportunity after Korea to surface. When in a tactical unit, you dedicated your time to the training of your men and that occupied every phase of your life both professionally and personally. The Army ROTC would reveal a paradox of professional cadre attempting to teach, train, mold and mentor young soldiers/Cadets/students in a liberal college environment. It was a period that taught tough lessons in politics and diplomacy to get the end result—a well-trained Second Lieutenant prepared to lead in the United States Army.

Life in the Army ROTC system revolved around recruiting potential cadets to receive classroom instruction and small doses of introduction to army tactical operations over the first two years. These were termed Military Science (MS) Level I and II Cadets. The big attraction for a student was a fairly easy and enjoyable class to bolster their grade point average with little effort. Extra credit was always offered to coax students to join the spring and fall Field Training Exercises. There they could play army while being led by the juniors and seniors as they prepared for their most crucial final training.

The juniors and seniors were termed MS III and MS IV cadets. All training for the first three years was meant to prepare a cadet for his biggest and most challenging test when he attended the Army ROTC Advanced Camp at Fort Lewis, WA; during the summer between his Junior and Senior years. There he would be evaluated and compete against all other MS III cadets across the nation for that year. He would then be ranked against with his peers and that ranking would judge his priority for preferences of a commissioning branch after his MS IV year.

For an ROTC program the biggest indicator of success or failure was the number of MS III Cadets who would attend and successfully complete Advanced Camp each year. From this number, you could forecast the final and most crucial number, which was the number of newly commissioned Second Lieutenants at the end of each school year. This number determined the viability and health of a program.

A typical program would have well over one hundred MS I and II Cadets. A healthy program would start the MS III year with close to twenty Cadets. Typically, the program would graduate around ten cadets each year. That number would be evaluated by the Army yearly and a new "mission" given for the next year. When I arrived at UNI, the program had graduated five cadets and the program had been put on its second probation. This meant the program had to show drastic improvement or it was in danger of being closed.

One of the first people I met when I arrived was MAJ Pat O'Reagan. He had been a UNI graduate many years earlier, spent time in Somalia, and was a great recruiter. He was a big man with an infectious personality, had a gift for gab, and was liked by all. MAJ O'Reagan had grown extremely frustrated with our program and was looking for anyway to expand our Cadet base on campus. We also had a National Guard MAJ Tony Cornelius who was very professional and was known and respected in the Iowa National Guard Community. Later, we were joined by Master Sergeant (MSG) Kevin Vann who had arrived from Korea and SFC Chabbotte our training NCO. Debbie Ackerson was the program secretary and very adept at managing the administrative requirements. With that team we set out to expand recruiting, improve training, and push the unit ahead.

The first year I taught the MS I and II students I tried to inspire by being approachable, professional, inspirational and engaging in athletics. I tried to make the class work interesting by including more current movies like *Gettysburg,* along with short clips of patrolling techniques from movies like *Predator* with Arnold Swarzenegger. Inspiring even one of these cadets to go on to the MS III level was as valuable as gold to the program.

During that first year we started with seven MS III Cadets, which meant our potential for success was very small. This could only be augmented by motivating completion cadets to finish the program. Completion Cadets were fifth-year students who had not graduated for one reason or another.

By the second year, through great recruiting, we started the year with twenty-two MS IIIs. This was the biggest number of cadets in any program within our region. To this point, no one had taken us seriously, and now we were the biggest program in the state. Of those twenty-two Cadets, eighteen completed Advanced Camp. As a result, the next year we commissioned fourteen Second Lieutenants. It was a very dramatic turn-around for the program and a credit to the team I have mentioned.

This did not come without a lot of extra effort from the staff. At 5 a.m. each day, I would take my Ford Bronco and make the rounds of my MS IIIs who had a problem of getting out of bed on time. I would go in their apartment and shake them out of bed, get them in the vehicle and haul them to Physical Training. The NCOs had an issue with coddling the Cadets. They felt if the cadet couldn't get to training, they didn't deserve to be commissioned. The officers did not agree as we all remembered the challenges of being a college student. The transition to the Officer Corps was a balance between college student and Cadet. One thing was certain: if the cadet did not graduate his studies with a degree he would never be commissioned.

It was during this tour that I learned that a Junior ROTC program had been offered to Crestwood High School in Cresco, Iowa. This was where I had gone to high school and I was excited they had the opportunity. A Junior ROTC program offers so many opportunities for young students looking to expand themselves and develop their character, personality, teamwork, and moral and ethical standards. Junior ROTC is a great program. Later I was told that Crestwood had declined the opportunity and I was extremely disappointed. There was a waiting list nationwide of schools wanting the program. To have been offered participation and then to decline it was a huge opportunity missed. I wondered what type of presentation they had received regarding the program because I could see no logical reason for declining the opportunity.

ROTC is a fantastic route for a soldier or student to be commissioned in any service. For an active duty Army officer, service as an ROTC instructor could be detrimental to your career. I was still motivated to return to the Ranger Regiment during this time so I continued to lift weights and road march consistently to stay in the best of shape. At 4 a.m. I would lift weights in the basements of my duplex while cranking Rob Zombie music. This environment fit my intensity level at the time. Then I would either bundle myself up in heavy sweats to do roadwork during the winter or head to the fitness center at the UNI Dome to run the stairs of the stadium. On some cold weather weekends I would run and road march the old UNI gymnasium stairs where the wrestling team worked out. I found their dedication most similar to what I was trying to accomplish and the coaches grew accustomed to seeing me huffing through the gym with a rucksack on my back. My opportunity finally presented itself in the fall of 1998. A position had become available at 1st Ranger Battalion, 75th Ranger Regiment, in Savannah, Georgia. The Battalion wanted me to take the job.

I approached LTC Colonel Dan Syhre, the UNI Professor of Military Science who refused to let me go. I then requested the Brigade Commander in Colorado authorize me to leave ROTC and take the job. He also refused, saying my mission at UNI ROTC was as important as the one with the Ranger Regiment. I was flabbergasted at the comparison of ROTC to the premier light infantry unit in the world. I had one last "blue chip" and asked for help from COL McChrystal, the 75th Ranger Regiment Commander. He personally called my Brigade Commander and requested I be released to return to duty with the Regiment. Again my Brigade Commander declined, and I had no other course to influence the decision. My opportunity was lost and my slot given to someone else.

This event was extremely disappointing and I became very disillusioned. Months of hard work seemed for nothing and even worse there would not be another opportunity for me to return to the Regiment. It was timing and relationships that brought you those opportunities and mine was gone.

Toward the end of my two-year tenure at UNI, I informed my superiors I wanted a job where I could deploy and get dirty again. In standard fashion, I was offered Recruiting and Reserves. My new wife encouraged me to hold fast and get a job that would challenge me and "recharge my batteries."

My telephone rang and when I picked it up I was greeted by my U.S. Army branch representative. He was sitting at his desk at the U.S. Army Personnel Command in Virginia. After a few pleasantries he asked if I would be interested in duty as a POW/MIA Team Leader. I was a bit surprised since I had little knowledge of the mission. I knew we attempted to recover our

POWs/MIAs, but had no idea of the scope of the operation. He explained that I would lead a team into Southeast Asia to locate and recover our missing POWs. My file was perfect for the job and he wanted to nominate me for the position. Assuming I passed an interview and approval process, I would be transferred to Hawaii to assume the post.

I was provided the name and telephone number of the Operations Director at Joint Task Force Full Accounting (JTF-FA), at Camp H.M. Smith, Hawaii. I dialed the number and when the telephone rang, I was greeted by LTC Mike Lerario who I was to contact for a telephonic interview. LTC Lerario answered the phone and explained I fit the minimum requirements of a Ranger Qualified, Command Qualified, and Combat Arms Captain. He was also pleased that I was a graduate of the Long Range Surveillance Leaders Course which he had also attended. LTC Lerario further explained that Ranger Officers were required to ensure the most tactically proficient and driven Team Leaders would ensure the completion of the mission. I fit the bill and we agreed to have me participate in one Joint Field Activity to Laos. I would participate as an observer to assess if I would be offered the job.

\*　　\*　　\*

# Never Leave a Fallen Comrade

On 8 May 2000, I departed for Hawaii and a new challenge that would be unlike any that I had experienced to this point in my career. I was headed to Southeast Asia in search of those Americans still missing from the war in Vietnam. I would lead over thirteen expeditions into the jungles of Laos and Cambodia to search forgotten battlefields for our missing comrades. These investigations would generate the adventure of a lifetime.

My time in search of our POW/MIAs lost in SEA generated more stories than I can tell in *Black Chinook.* Would I recount the discovery of the Green Beret who was shot in the chest, immediately after insertion, and buried by the locals? We found his grave in the center of a grove of trees riddled by a firefight years ago. Maybe the story of how we discovered an O-2 Spotter plane along a river in Xekong Province. We were searching for its cowboy boot-wearing pilot who ignored heavy ground fire to control an air strike on a Vietnamese convoy. He was shot down and buried on a grassy knoll. We found him. Perhaps tell the story of flying to Kotang Island off the Cambodian coast. We searched there for Marines missing after an amphibious landing to rescue the hostages from the Mayaguez Incident. They fought a fruitless battle to hold the beach while other helicopters crashed into the ocean during the final approach. These events deserve a detailed description to do justice to the heroism of the men who were lost, and my team who risked everything to find them. It was our mission to bring them home.

I decided to tell the stories of that chapter in my career in a book called, *Thick Luck – The Search for America's POWs and*

*MIAs.* The Lao and Cambodian villagers called us "Bone Hunters." The strange men who would arrive out without warning and trek into the jungle in search of the dead. We were not bone hunters—we were military experts on a mission to find our fallen comrades who had fallen into the hands of the enemy. We would go to any length to find them ... we did ... we brought them home. Look for *"Thick Luck"* to read these stories of our expeditions to search forgotten battlefields in Laos and Cambodia.

# Glossary

## Abbreviations/Acronyms

| | |
|---|---|
| 1SG | First Sergeant |
| A-10 | Thunderbolt Tank Buster |
| ABN | Airborne |
| AC-130 | Spectre Gunship |
| AH-6 | Little Bird helicopter |
| AIT | Advanced Individual Training |
| ARS | Army Reception Station |
| ASVAB | Army Service Vocational Aptitude Battery |
| BABC | Ban Alang Base Camp |
| BDU | Basic Duty Uniform |
| BLU-43 | Dragon Tooth anti-personnel mine |
| BMP | Tracked Russian armored personnel carrier |
| BRDM | Wheeled Russian armored personnel carrier |
| BT | Basic Training |
| C-130 | Hercules transport plane |
| C-141 | Star lifter transport plane |
| CH-47 | Chinook helicopter (cargo/troops) |
| CH-53 | Pavlo helicopter (cargo/troops) |
| CAR-15 | Carbine Assault Rifle |
| COL | Colonel |
| COLT | Combat Observation Lasing Teams |
| CPH | Copper Head laser guided artillery round |
| CPT | Captain |
| CO | Commanding Officer |
| DAP | Direct Action Penetrater (MH-60 Helicopter) |
| DIA | Defense Intelligence Agency |
| DivArty | Division Artillery |
| DPMO | Defense POW/MIA Office |
| DZSO | Drop Zone Safety Officer |

| | |
|---|---|
| FIST | Fire Support Team |
| FO | Forward Observer |
| FRAGO | Fragmentation Order |
| FSB | Forward Staging Base |
| FSO | Fire Support Officer |
| FTX | Field Training Exercise |
| G/LVVD | Ground Vehicular Laser Locator Designator |
| GTMO | Guantanamo Bay, Cuba |
| HALO/ | High Altitude Low Opening/High Altitude High |
| HAHO | Opening |
| HIND-D | Russian Attack Helicopter |
| ID | Infantry Division |
| IE | Investigative Element |
| ISB | Initial Staging Base |
| JMPI | Jumpmaster Parachute Inspection |
| JFA | Joint Field Activity |
| JOTC | Jungle Operations Training Center |
| JRTC | Joint Readiness Training Center |
| JSOC | Joint Special Operations Command |
| JTF-FA | Joint Task Force Full Accounting |
| KILO | Impact area on Fort Benning, GA |
| LAW | Light Anti-tank Weapon |
| LBE | Load Bearing Equipment |
| LCM | Mechanized Load Carrying Assault Boat (Navy) |
| LCOL | Lieutenant Colonel |
| LNO | Liaison Officer |
| LPL-30 | Laser Pointer |
| LRRP | Long Range Recon Patrol |
| LRSLC | Long Range Surveillance Leader Course |
| LTC | Lieutenant Colonel |
| LZ | Landing Zone |
| M-1950 | Weapons carrying case (airborne) |
| M-2 | .50 cal Machine Gun |

| | |
|---|---|
| M-203 | Grenade launcher |
| M240G | 7.62 machine gun |
| M-60 | 7.62 machine gun |
| MAJ | Major |
| MFFJM | Military Freefall Jumpmaster |
| MG | Major General |
| MIA | Missing In Action |
| MK-19 | Grenade launcher |
| MOUT | Military Operations in Urban Terrain |
| MP | Military Police |
| M-577 | Armored Command Post vehicle |
| MTT | Mobile Training Team |
| NCO | Non-Commissioned Officer |
| NCOIC | Non-Commissioned Officer In Charge |
| NTC | National Training Center |
| NVG | Night vision goggles |
| OCS | Officer Candidate School |
| OIC | Officer in Charge |
| OPFOR | Opposing Forces |
| OPORD | Operations Order |
| PFC | Private First Class |
| PL | Platoon Leader |
| POMCUS | Pre-positioning of Material Configured in Unit Sets |
| POW | Prisoner Of War |
| PT | Physical Training |
| PVS-7 | Night Vision Goggles |
| PZ | Pick-up Zone |
| RE | Recovery Element |
| REFORGER | Return of Forces to Germany |
| RI | Ranger Instructor |
| RIP | Ranger Indoctrination Program |
| ROTC | Reserve Officer Training Corp |

| | |
|---|---|
| RRF1 | Ranger Readiness Force One |
| RSOV | Ranger Special Operations Vehicle |
| RTO | Radio and Telephone Operator |
| S-3 | Operations Officer |
| SAS | Special Air Services |
| SAW | Squad Automatic Weapon |
| SDO | Staff Duty Officer |
| SF | Special Forces |
| SFC | Sergeant First Class (E7) |
| SGT | Sergeant (E5) |
| SITREP | Situation Report |
| SOP | Standard Operating Procedures |
| SPIE | Small Patrol Infiltration or Exfiltration Rig |
| SSG | Staff Sergeant (E6) |
| SWC | Special Warfare Center |
| T-55 | Russian Tank |
| TOC | Tactical Operations Center |
| TVD | Tennessee Valley Divide |
| U(M)H-60 | Black hawk helicopter |
| UXO | Unexploded Ordnance |

# About the Author

Major David A. Combs entered the United States Army on 22 August 1985. He attended Basic Training and Advanced Individual Training at Fort Sill, Oklahoma. He graduated from the Officer Candidate School and was commissioned a Second Lieutenant in 1991.

Major Combs assignments included: Fire Support Sergeant, 3/75 Ranger Battalion, Senior Fire Support Sergeant 75th Ranger Regiment, Fort Benning, GA;, Colt Team Leader and Battalion Fire Support Officer at 3/29 Field Artillery, 4th ID, Fort Carson, CO; C-Company 2/75 Ranger Battalion, Fire Support Officer, Fort Lewis, WA; Battery Commander 1-15th Field Artillery, 2nd Infantry Division, Camp Casey, Korea; Army ROTC Instructor, University of Northern Iowa, Cedar Falls, IA; POW/MIA Team Leader, Joint Task Force Full Accounting, Camp H.M. Smith, HI; Assistant S-3, 25th ID(L) DivArty, Schofield Barracks, HI; Strategic Planner, Combined Forces Command Afghanistan.

His military and civilian education include: Bachelor of Science Degree, Officer Candidate School, Field Artillery Officer Basic Course, Field Artillery Officer Advance Course, Command and General Staff College. Military Schools include: Ranger, Pathfinder, Air Assault, Airborne, and Military Free Fall.

Awards include: the Bronze Star Medal, Defense Meritorious Service Medal, Meritorious Service Medal (2), Army Commendation Medal (6), Joint Service Achievement Medal (3), Army Achievement Medal (6), Armed Forces Expeditionary Medal (2) with Arrowhead Device and Bronze Service Star, Humanitarian Service Medal, Global War On Terrorism Service Medal, Global War On Terrorism Expeditionary Medal, Afghanistan Campaign Medal, and Bronze Service Star (Combat Parachute Jump).

He now continues to serve the United States military as a contractor in both Afghanistan and Iraq.